Cambridge English
First
Practice Tests

Four tests for the Cambridge English: First exam

MARK HARRISON

OXFORD
UNIVERSITY PRESS

ACKNOWLEDGEMENTS

*The author and publisher are grateful to those who have given permission to reproduce
the following extracts and adaptations of copyright material:*

p.6 Extract from 'Multitasking children are losing the plot' by John Elliott,
The Sunday Times, 26 March 2006. Reproduced by permission of NI
Syndication.

p.10 Extract from 'Hi, anxiety' by Tiffany Hancock, The Telegraph, 17
January 2006 www.telegraph.co.uk. © Telegraph Media Group Limited 2006.
Reproduced by permission.

p.12 Extract from 'Want to join the jet set?' by Linda Whitney, The Daily
Mail, 30 March 2006. Reproduced by permission of Solo Syndication.

p.15 Extract adapted from 'The best-seller's book club' by Lesley Jones and
Ophelia Zwart, Eve Magazine, May 2005. Reproduced by permission of
Haymarket Media Group.

p.20 Extract from 'A Life in Sport: The Duke of Argyll Elephant Polo' by
Sarah Edworthy, The Telegraph, 29 November 2006. © Telegraph Media
Group Limited 2006. Reproduced by permission.

p.26 Extract from 'A shopping revolution' by Natasha Perry from p.17,
Hendon & Finchley Times 16 March 2006. Reproduced by permission of
Newsquest London Ltd.

p.30 Adapted from 'A Gathering Light' by Jennifer Donnelly, A&C Black
Publishers, an imprint of Bloomsbury Publishing PLC and 'A Northern Light'
by Jennifer Donnelly. Copyright © 2003 by Jennifer Donnelly. Used by
permission of Houghton Mifflin Harcourt Publishing Company. All rights
reserved.

p.32 Extract from 'The tower and the glory' by Chris Wilson, The Telegraph,
10 September 2005. © Telegraph Media Group Limited 2005. Reproduced by
permission.

p.35 Extract from 'Wheels that changed the world' by Nick Horley, The Daily
Mail, 9 May 2005. Reproduced by permission of Solo Syndication.

p.39 Extract from 'Power to the people' by David Derbyshire, The Telegraph,
4 November 2006. © Telegraph Media Group Limited 2006. Reproduced by
permission.

p.46 Extract from 'See the New Car in the Joneses' Driveway? You May
Soon Be Driving One Just Like It' by David Leonhardt, from The New York
Times, 13 June 2005 © 2005 The New York Times. All rights reserved. Used

by permission and protected by the Copyright Laws of the United States. The
printing, copying, redistribution, or retransmission of this Content without
express written permission is prohibited.

p.50 Extract from 'Are you on the right track? How to find a career that
fits your personality' by Frances Childs, The Telegraph, 18 August 2005.
© Telegraph Media Group Limited 2005. Reproduced by permission.

p.52 Extract from 'Strike out with street fighting class' from p.15 Hendon
& Finchley Times 9 March 2006. Reproduced by permission of Newsquest
London Ltd.

p.55 Extract from 'Smart art' by Sean Newson in The Sunday Times, 19 June
2005. Reproduced by permission of NI Syndication.

p.62 Extract from 'Our girls are alive with the *Sound of Music*' by Hugh Davies,
The Telegraph 14 October 2006. © Telegraph Media Group Limited 2006.
Reproduced by permission.

p.66 Extract from 'She's Studying. He's Playing' by John Schwartz, The New
York Times, 14 June 2005 © 2005 The New York Times. All rights reserved.
Used by permission and protected by the Copyright Laws of the United
States. The printing, copying, redistribution, or retransmission of this
Content without express written permission is prohibited.

p.68 Extract from 'Itineraries; Grading the C.E.O. Speech' by Sharon
McDonnell, The New York Times, 27 September 2005 © 2005 The New
York Times. All rights reserved. Used by permission and protected by the
Copyright Laws of the United States. The printing, copying, redistribution,
or retransmission of this Content without express written permission is
prohibited.

p.70 Extract from 'Why I've taken a break from holidays' by Tom Cox,
The Telegraph 18 August 2005. © Telegraph Media Group Limited 2005.
Reproduced by permission.

p.72 Extract from 'Please Don't Touch the Celebrities' by Patricia Leigh
Brown, The New York Times, 2 March 2006 © 2006 The New York Times. All
rights reserved. Used by permission and protected by the Copyright Laws of
the United States. The printing, copying, redistribution, or retransmission of
this Content without express written permission is prohibited.

p.75 Extract from 'Baseball's Origins: They Ain't Found Till They're Found'
by Bill Pennington, The New York Times, 12 September 2004 © 2004 The
New York Times. All rights reserved. Used by permission and protected
by the Copyright Laws of the United States. The printing, copying,
redistribution, or retransmission of this Content without express written
permission is prohibited.

p.78 Extract from '24 Hours in Food' by Kate Salter, The Sunday Times,
September 2006. Reproduced by permission of NI Syndication.

p.78 Adapted extract from 'Piers Morgan meets … Johnny Depp,' Issue 29
17–23 November 2006 www.FirstNews.co.uk. Reproduced by permission of
FirstNews.

p.79 Extract from 'Dashboard dunces exposed' by Sally Pook, The Telegraph
3 March 2006. © Telegraph Media Group Limited 2006. Reproduced by
permission.

p.80 Extract from 'Change your life in 60 seconds' by Louise Armistead, The
Sunday Times, 19 June 2005. Reproduced by permission of NI Syndication.

p.82 Extract from "You can CY" Taken from Angel Magazine July 2006, www.
angelmagazine.co.uk. Reproduced by permission of Archant Community
Media Ltd.

*Although every effort has been made to trace and contact copyright holders before
publication, this has not been possible in some cases. We apologise for any apparent
infringement of copyright and, if notified, the publisher will be pleased to rectify any
errors or omissions at the earliest possible opportunity.*

*The publisher would like to thank the following for their kind permission to
reproduce photographs:* Alamy pp.12 (XiXinXing), 24 (Modern house/Gregg
Vignal), 24 (Girl/OlegMit), 24 (Boys/RichardBaker), 44 (Skyfall/Photos 12),
55 (Archivart), 64 (Graduates/Blend Images), 72 (Arcaid Images), 84 (Coach/
John Powell Photographer), 84 (Backpackers/Andrew Woodley); 84 (Working
from home/Tetra Images), Getty Images pp.24 (Messy room/Photofusion),
52 (tunart), 64 (Business people/A. Chederros), 64 (Businessmen/Stockbyte),
75 (Skip ODonnell), 84 (Modern office/Nick David); Oxford University Press
pp.44 (Professional kitchen/Oxford University Press), 44 (Family cooking/
Karina Mansfield); Rex Features p.44 (Escape from Planet Earth/Snap Stills);
shutterstock pp.34 (KarSol), 64 (Tourist/Ekaterina Pokrovsky); The Random
House Group Ltd. p.15 (Jeff Cottenden)

Tables on pp.94 and 95 reproduced with permission of Cambridge English
Language Assessment © 2014

Access a self-study online extract from a Cambridge English: First
test at www.oxfordenglishtesting.com
Unlock code: ad3c53-8c2a96-dca35b-5ffcb3

Contents

Introduction   4

TEST 1

Reading and Use of English   6
Writing   16
Listening   18
Speaking   23

TEST 2

Reading and Use of English   26
Writing   36
Listening   38
Speaking   43

TEST 3

Reading and Use of English   46
Writing   56
Listening   58
Speaking   63

TEST 4

Reading and Use of English   66
Writing   76
Listening   78
Speaking   83

Answer sheets   86
Assessing the Writing paper   94
Assessing the Speaking paper   95

Introduction

This book contains:

- four print practice tests for the Cambridge English: First exam (2015)
- guidance on how to assess the Writing and Speaking papers
- answer sheets

Exam content

Reading and Use of English (1 hour 15 minutes)

	Text / Input	Question type	Focus
PART 1	1 short text with 8 gaps	4-option multiple-choice; choose the correct word(s) to fill each gap	vocabulary (e.g. idioms, collocations, completion of phrases, phrasal verbs, etc.) **8 questions; 8 marks**
PART 2	1 short text with 8 gaps	fill each gap with one word	mostly grammar, some vocabulary **8 questions; 8 marks**
PART 3	1 short text with 8 gaps	use the words given to form the correct word for each gap	word formation **8 questions; 8 marks**
PART 4	6 unrelated sentences, each followed by a single word and a gapped sentence	use the word given to complete the gapped sentence so that it means the same as the first sentence	grammar, vocabulary, collocation **6 questions; 12 marks** *(each correct answer receives up to 2 marks)*
PART 5	1 text	4-option multiple choice	comprehension of detail, opinion, attitude, purpose, gist, meaning from context, implication, reference, exemplification, main idea, tone **6 questions; 12 marks**
PART 6	1 text with 6 sentences missing	choice of 7 sentences to fill the gaps	understanding of text structure, links between parts of text, global meaning **6 questions; 12 marks**
PART 7	1 text divided into sections OR several short texts	matching statements / information to section of text or short text they refer to or appear in	comprehension of specific information, detail, opinion, implication **10 questions; 10 marks**

Writing (1 hour 20 minutes)

	Task	Focus
PART 1	essay, responding to given title and using given ideas and an idea of their own for content (140–190 words) Candidates **must** do this task.	expressing and giving reasons for an opinion
PART 2	article, report, review, email or letter (140–190 words) Candidates choose one task from three choices.	varying according to the task, including advising, comparing, describing, explaining, expressing opinions, justifying, recommending

Listening (40 minutes)

In the exam, each recording is heard twice. On the CD, Parts 2, 3 and 4 are not repeated and the track will need to be played again. At the end of the exam, candidates are given 5 minutes to transfer their answers to the answer sheet.

	Recording	Question type	Focus
PART 1	8 short pieces (monologue or conversation)	3-option multiple-choice (1 question per piece)	genre, identifying speaker feeling, attitude, opinion, purpose, agreement between speakers, gist, detail **8 questions; 8 marks**
PART 2	1 monologue	sentence completion: 10 sentences to complete with a word or short phrase	understanding of specific information, detail, stated opinion **10 questions; 10 marks**
PART 3	5 short monologues	matching: match what each speaker says to 1 of 8 options	identifying attitude, opinion, gist, purpose, feeling, main points, detail **5 questions; 5 marks**
PART 4	1 interview or conversation (2 speakers)	3-option multiple-choice	identifying opinion, attitude, detail, gist, main idea, specific information **7 questions; 7 marks**

Speaking (14 minutes)

	Activity type (examiner + two candidates)	Focus
PART 1	conversation between candidates and examiner (2 mins)	general interaction, social language
PART 2	individual 'long turn' for each candidate with a brief response from second candidate (4 mins)	comparing, describing, expressing opinions
PART 3	discussion between candidates followed by a decision-making task (4 mins)	exchanging ideas, expressing and justifying opinions, agreeing/disagreeing, suggesting, speculating, evaluating, negotiating
PART 4	conversation between candidates and examiner (4 mins)	expressing and justifying opinions, agreeing/disagreeing, speculating

The Reading and Use of English paper carries 40% of the total. The Writing, Listening and Speaking papers each carry 20% of the total.

Reading and Use of English (1 hour 15 minutes)

PART 1

For questions 1–8, read the text below and decide which answer (A, B, C or D) best fits each gap. There is an example at the beginning (0).

Mark your answers on the separate answer sheet.

Example:

0 **A** seriously   **B** extremely   **C** absolutely   **D** intensely

0	**A**	B	C	D

Multitasking children

The trend for children to multitask by juggling all sorts of electronic gadgets at the same time is **0** _____________ damaging their levels of concentration, scientists have warned. They found that children **1** _____________ homework while sending messages via the Internet can **2** _____________ up spending 50% longer than if they had done each task **3** _____________.

David E Meyer, Professor of Cognitive Psychology at the University of Michigan, said that true multitasking is **4** _____________ possible for simple activities such as ironing and listening to the radio. He ran experiments demonstrating that young adults who had to **5** _____________ from one maths problem to another wasted significant amounts of time. Meyer said: 'For situations **6** _____________ more complex tasks, especially those requiring language, the total time taken to get all the tasks done will increase **7** _____________ . Over long periods, this kind of multitasking can stress you out and **8** _____________ to mental and physical exhaustion.'

1	**A** engaging	**B** tackling	**C** attending	**D** undergoing
2	**A** turn	**B** come	**C** use	**D** end
3	**A** separately	**B** distinctly	**C** apart	**D** aside
4	**A** merely	**B** purely	**C** only	**D** simply
5	**A** alter	**B** switch	**C** interrupt	**D** exchange
6	**A** consisting	**B** containing	**C** involving	**D** meaning
7	**A** largely	**B** greatly	**C** widely	**D** highly
8	**A** result	**B** proceed	**C** lead	**D** bring

PART 2

For questions **9–16**, *read the text below and think of the word which best fits each gap. Use only* **one** *word in each gap. There is an example at the beginning (* **0** *).*

Write your answers IN CAPITAL LETTERS on the separate answer sheet.

Example:

| 0 | I | T | | | | | | | | | | | |

The London Marathon

The London Marathon race is a long-running story. **0**___________ was first held in 1981,

9___________ when more than half a million marathon runners of various shapes, sizes and abilities have completed the challenge of running the full 42 km of the course.

    The London Marathon was the brainchild of Chris Brasher. The former Olympic champion brought the idea home to London **10**___________ completing the New York Marathon in 1979. 'Could London stage **11**___________ an event?' wondered Brasher, answering his **12**___________ question by organizing the first London Marathon on March 29 1981, **13**___________ 6,255 runners completed the course.

    The event has captured the public imagination and there are always **14**___________ many people wanting to take part. Last year **15**___________ amazing 98,500 people applied to run in it, although only 46,500 **16**___________ be accepted.

    For those who do take part, the day is about fun, achievement and raising money for charity – with varying degrees of pain!

For questions 17–24, read the text below. Use the word given in capitals at the end of some of the lines to form a word that fits in the gap in the same line. There is an example at the beginning (0).

Write your answers IN CAPITAL LETTERS on the separate answer sheet.

Example:

| 0 | N | A | T | I | O | N | A | L | | | | | |

MOBILE LIBRARY'S A WINNER

The city's new mobile library has won an award at a **0** __________ meeting   **NATION**

of mobile library providers. The award is for the **17** __________ design of   **STAND**

this new vehicle.

    The new library went into **18** __________ in April and has been very well   **SERVE**

received by the public. Both visits and loans of books have increased

19 __________ since the new vehicle began operating. Comments have   **CONSIDER**

included 'It's such a friendly-looking library', 'I couldn't wait to look

inside!' and 'Thanks for all the **20** __________ new books.'   **WONDER**

    The mobile library is an air-conditioned, state-of-the-art vehicle, which is

fully networked for using information technology. The air suspension system

allows the vehicle to be **21** __________ for easy access and ensures   **LOW**

22 __________ when parked. The internal layout was designed with major   **STABLE**

input from the library staff, who insisted that the décor was bright and

23 __________ . The library carries up to 3,000 books, CDs and DVDs for   **COLOUR**

all ages and **24** __________ , and much of the stock is brand new.   **INTERESTED**

For questions 25–30, complete the second sentence so that it has a similar meaning to the first sentence, using the word given. Do not change the word given. You must use between two and five words, including the word given. Here is an example (0).

Example:

0   Making new friends was easy for her.

DIFFICULT

She didn't _________________ new friends.

The gap can be filled with the words 'find it difficult to make', so you write:

0	FIND IT DIFFICULT TO MAKE

Write only the missing words IN CAPITAL LETTERS on the separate answer sheet.

---

25 Despite winning the race, he wasn't very pleased.

EVEN

He wasn't very pleased, _________________ the race.

26 His first novel was better than this one.

GOOD

This novel is not _________________ one he wrote.

27 I'm sorry, could you wait for a moment, please?

MIND

I'm sorry, _________________ for a moment, please?

28 We're so late now that we definitely won't get to the party on time.

CHANCE

We're so late that we have _________________ to the party on time.

29 The food she eats affects her health badly.

EFFECT

The food she eats _________________ her health.

30 The only thing I did at the weekend was housework.

APART

I did _________________ housework at the weekend.

You are going to read a newspaper article about an adventure centre. For questions 31–36, choose the answer (A, B, C or D) which you think fits best according to the text.

Mark your answers on the separate answer sheet.

A family adventure centre

I'm focused. Completely terrified, but focused. I've got a tiny area to stand on and beneath me is a 10-metre drop. To make things worse, the totem pole that I'm trying to climb onto is shaking. With one knee bent on the top of the pole and the other foot next to it, I slowly stand up with my arms outstretched for balance. Once upright, my legs are still wobbling but an enormous smile has spread across my face. I shuffle my toes over the edge. And then I jump. Back on the ground, my knees won't stop quaking. But for the boys at Head 4 Heights, an aerial adventure centre in Cirencester, it's all in a day's work.

Head 4 Heights, one of the tallest climbing centres in Britain, opened two years ago. It's the only UK climbing centre open to the public year-round (the only days it closes are when winds exceed 70 mph, almost enough to blow you off a totem pole and into one of the lakes). The course was set up by Rod Baber, adventurer extraordinaire and holder of the world record for scaling the highest peak of every country in Europe in the shortest time. Rod's latest plan is to snag the record for North and South America as well, but in between he starts every day with a clamber round the Cirencester course.

Although the course is only roughly the size of a tennis court, it packs a lot into a small space. There are four totem poles (of varying degrees of difficulty according to the holds attached to them), a stairway to heaven (a giant ladder with an increasing distance between the rungs), two freefall platforms and a trapeze jump. Plans for a new 30-metre pole are presently under way. All can be made easier or harder, according to ability, and incorporated into different challenges, which is why the course has proved a success with families, corporate days out and the armed forces. More than half who visit return for more and the centre now averages about 1,500 visitors a month.

All ages over five are welcome, but children are the most enthusiastic and 'far easier to teach than the bankers,' says Rod. Parents are usually more reluctant to join in. 'We hear all sorts of excuses,' says Rod. 'Everything from bad knees to "I haven't trimmed my toenails".' The oldest customer was a 78-year-old who arrived with his son and grandson. When the younger two decided to give it a miss, the grandfather set off to show them how it was done.

For the most part, though, people start off nervous and only gain confidence as they progress. 'Everything is kept very positive. We always tell people to look up not down and to take their time,' says Rod. 'We want to push people outside their comfort zone and into the adventure zone, but we don't want people to be pushed into the panic zone, which can be mentally damaging.'

Also reassuring is the 100 per cent safety record. The course was designed and built by Nick Moriarty, an expert in his field who has constructed 450 courses in 16 countries and trained 2,700 instructors. Key to the design is the safety-rope system, which ensures that if you do lose your balance or grip, your full-body harness will guarantee that you float, not fall, back to earth.

31 One problem the writer describes in the first paragraph is that

    A she keeps falling off the totem pole.
    B she is trying to stand on top of a moving object.
    C she cannot get her arms into the right position.
    D she is too nervous to complete the climb.

31

32 What do we learn about Head 4 Heights in the second paragraph?

    A It remains open even in quite windy conditions.
    B Rod Baber got the idea for it while climbing mountains.
    C It did not initially stay open throughout the year.
    D It is aimed at people who don't have the chance to climb mountains.

32

33 The writer says that the main reason for the course's popularity is that

    A the challenges it offers cannot be found anywhere else.
    B new challenges are constantly being added.
    C it can be completed in a fairly short time.
    D it can be adapted for different people.

33

34 The people who 'decided to give it a miss' (column 3) are examples of people who

    A find it difficult to do the course.
    B are unwilling to do the course.
    C are easily taught how to do the course.
    D give up while they are doing course.

34

35 Rod says that the intention of the course is that people taking part

    A learn how to deal with extreme fear.
    B progress as quickly as possible.
    C take risks they might not initially want to take.
    D increase in confidence after repeated visits.

35

36 The writer uses the phrase 'Also reassuring' (column 3) to emphasize

    A that people benefit from doing the course.
    B how carefully the course has been constructed.
    C that people should not be afraid to do the course.
    D how enthusiastic Rod is about the course.

36

PART 6

You are going to read an article about jobs that involve international travel. Six sentences have been removed from the article. Choose from the sentences A–G the one which fits each gap (37–42). There is one extra sentence which you do not need to use.

Mark your answers on the separate answer sheet.

WANT TO JOIN THE JET SET?

You could be jetting off to exotic locations, staying in five-star hotels, eating in top-class restaurants, and it's all paid for by your employer. Who wouldn't want a job that involves foreign travel? **37** ___________ The number of jobs requiring international travel is growing significantly. And citing business travel experience on your CV can bring enormous professional benefits.

But it's not always as exciting as it sounds. There is a big difference between travelling to Milan as a tourist and travelling there to spend a day in the type of hotel meeting room that can be found anywhere in Europe. It can be very exciting, but you need to keep your feet firmly on the ground. **38** ___________ Flights can be delayed, things can go wrong and it's easy to get exhausted. Many jobs mean travelling alone, so you can be lonely.

Simply targeting any job that involves foreign travel is not the way to start. Instead, you should consider all the usual factors, such as qualifications and experience, and only then choose a sector or company that offers opportunities for international travel. The travel and hotel trades are obvious areas, but the commercial sector also offers good prospects for travel. In the retail sector, buyers often travel, especially if they work in fresh produce, where they have to check the suitability of crops. **39** ___________ Jobs in the engineering and environment sector can involve travel, too. Almost any career can mean international travel, if you choose the right company and role. The number of jobs involving travel, especially at middle-management level, is growing.

So what will help you secure a role with an international flavour? **40** ___________ A second language is a good indication of how well someone will adapt. You need to show you are flexible and willing to learn. If your company has a sister company in the Czech Republic, for instance, learning some Czech will boost your chances.

Find out what the company offers as a support package. Many now guarantee that you can return home at the weekends, or they will limit the amount that people travel each year. **41** ___________ One company asked graduates fresh out of university to move to another country over a weekend, alone, and to find their own accommodation.

And it's as well to remember that international travel can be stressful. People can get burned out by international business travel. You need to be in control of your schedule, rather than leaving it to the company. You must ensure you get time to rest and talk to your employer all the time about how you are coping. Don't wait for formal appraisals or until they ask for your views. **42** ___________ Most sensible companies ask people to commit to two to three years. This increases the likelihood of success. And most people who travel on business remember it fondly.

A On the other hand, it does bring personal benefits, and it also has a dramatic effect on promotion prospects.

B And realize you might not want to travel for ever.

C Employers look for candidates with an international outlook.

D And there are plenty of opportunities.

E But not all employers are like this.

F Speak to seasoned international business travellers to get an idea of what you will face.

G Employment in communications, banking and finance, and property management is also worth looking at.

PART 7

You are going to read a magazine article about various authors. For questions 43–52, choose from the authors (A–D). The authors may be chosen more than once.

Mark your answers on the separate answer sheet.

Which author

took action in response to someone's negative view of her chances of getting her work accepted? **43**

decides when information given in her books does not have to be true? **44**

did something dishonest while trying to get her work accepted? **45**

was offered her first contract as a result of an earlier success? **46**

makes sure that her books contain strange elements? **47**

draws attention to the likelihood of a new author getting their work accepted? **48**

wants people to be cheered up by her books? **49**

feels that it is an advantage that people give her their sincere views on her work? **50**

recommends analysing various aspects of other authors' books? **51**

felt that her job was taking up too much of her attention? **52**

The best-sellers book club

Fancy being an author? We asked some of Britain's favourite best-selling writers to share the secrets of their success.

A JOANNE HARRIS *Her novels have attracted millions of fans worldwide.*

MY BIG BREAK I was a full-time teacher and made time to write my first novel before and after school. It took two years. Then I spent a fortune on posting manuscripts to agents. I found one, but he got discouraged when my manuscripts were rejected, so I sacked him and wrote my next novel, which my next agent loved. He got me a deal for both novels.

MY BEST ADVICE 100,000 titles are published in the UK every year. For each, 100 are rejected. If, knowing this, you still want to write and you love it, you're on the right track.

THE SECRET OF MY SUCCESS I don't believe in a magic wand. You need ability, luck and hard work.

B LAUREN CHILD *She writes and illustrates children's books for 2 to 10-year-olds.*

MY BIG BREAK After school, I did an art course. Then I did all sorts of jobs – making lampshades, working as an assistant to artist Damien Hirst (I painted a lot of the spots on his paintings). I wrote my first book in the hope it would become an animation. I found an agent, but didn't get a deal for five years. I didn't lose heart, as so many people were positive about it. Eventually I got a deal and was asked to do a second book.

MY BEST ADVICE Read as much as you can before you even think of writing. And you can't please everyone – above all, your work must interest you.

THE SECRET OF MY SUCCESS I keep stories simple, but always add a quirky touch – children really like the more bizarre moments in life. I also have a very honest audience who tell me what they think.

C FREYA NORTH *She writes lively, fast-paced fiction.*

MY BIG BREAK I was doing a PhD in Art History and bought a computer. The sheer joy of typing then deleting stuff was compulsive and I started to write fiction that I actually wanted to read. After four years of rejections, I presumed I was doing something wrong. Then I worked for a publishing company and realized I needed an agent. I sent my manuscript with fake reviews I'd made up myself to lots of agents. One took me on and got me a three-book deal.

MY BEST ADVICE Let your character dictate the story. It could be the most intricate plot in the world, but if the characters aren't 'real', no one will care.

THE SECRET OF MY SUCCESS I write simply and keep chapters short so my readers can enjoy them on journeys home at the end of a bad day. I want them to giggle.

D MANDA SCOTT *She has written a cult series of historical novels.*

MY BIG BREAK I was a veterinary anaesthetist. On my 30th birthday, I was climbing a mountain and I was happy, but all I could think about was work on Monday. I decided to follow my heart and make a living from writing. I was among the finalists in a writing competition and from that got a deal for my first book.

MY BEST ADVICE Read bad books and work out what makes them bad. Read the books you love and work out why you love them. Write what you will really, really want to read. Always.

THE SECRET OF MY SUCCESS I'm good at judging what needs to be factual and what I can make up.

Writing (1 hour 20 minutes)

PART 1

*You **must** answer this question. Write your answer in **140–190** words in an appropriate style.*

1   In your English class you have been talking about computer games and the effects they have on people who play them. Now, your English teacher has asked you to write an essay.

Write an essay using **all** the notes and give reasons for your point of view.

> Computer games are very bad for people and they cause a lot of problems.
> Do you agree?
>
> **Notes**
> Write about:
> 1.   time spent playing the games
> 2.   feelings they give to people
> 3.   __________________ (your own idea)

PART 2

*Write an answer to **one** of the questions **2–4** in this part. Write your answer in **140–190** words in an appropriate style.*

---

2   You are going to visit Britain for three weeks in the near future. You have received an email from a British friend, Olivia. Read this part of Olivia's email and then write your email to Mr and Mrs Hampson.

> While you're here, you could stay with some relatives of mine (Joe and Lisa Hampson) who live in the Midlands. I've spoken to them and they'd be pleased to put you up for a few days. I think you should write to them (address below), tell them about yourself and your plans, and ask for information about what you can do there.

Write your **email**.

3   You have seen this announcement in an international magazine.

> ### PERFORMING IN PUBLIC
>
> Tell us about your experience of performing or speaking in public. What did you do and where? How did it go? Was it a success or a disaster? And how did you feel?
>
> We'll publish the best articles in a special section next month.

Write your **article**.

4   You recently saw this notice in an English-language magazine.

> ### WHAT DON'T YOU LIKE ON TV?
>
> Is there a programme on TV that you really dislike? We're looking for reviews of programmes you really can't stand. Tell us what you don't like about the programme and we'll publish the angriest reviews!

Write your **review**.

Listening (40 minutes)

PART 1

You will hear people talking in eight different situations. For questions 1–8, choose the best answer, (A, B or C).

1 You hear someone talking about football referees.
   What is the speaker's attitude towards referees?

   A They make too many mistakes.

   B They deserve sympathy.

   C Some are better than others.

   `1`

2 You hear a famous chef talking about his week.
   What does he say about what happened during the week?

   A He had a problem that was not his fault.

   B He didn't want to appear on so many programmes.

   C He had his first experience of live TV.

   `2`

3 You hear someone talking about her career in dancing.
   What does she emphasize?

   A the contribution made by her parents

   B how much hard work she did

   C her desire to be a dancer

   `3`

4 You hear someone talking on the phone at work.
   Who is she talking to?

   A a colleague

   B her boss

   C a client

   `4`

5   You hear a radio presenter talking about a book.
    What feeling does the presenter express about the book?

    A   doubt that it does exactly what it says it does

    B   amazement at how up to date its information is

    C   curiosity about how it was written

5

6   You hear part of an interview with a famous comedian.
    What does he say about his school days?

    A   The teachers never criticized him.

    B   He was only good at one subject.

    C   Other people found him amusing.

6

7   You hear someone talking about a person he knows.
    What is the speaker doing?

    A   complaining

    B   apologizing

    C   arguing

7

8   You hear a tour guide talking to a group of visitors to a museum.
    What does he tell them about the museum?

    A   It's easy to get lost in it.

    B   Big groups aren't allowed in some parts of it.

    C   It's better only to visit a small part of it.

8

PART 2

You will hear someone talking about the sport of elephant polo. For questions 9–18, complete the sentences with a word or short phrase.

ELEPHANT POLO

Elephants are **9** ______________________________ animals and so they enjoy elephant polo.

The **10** ______________________________ of a goal in elephant polo is the same as in football.

A player and an elephant **11** ______________________________ both sit on each elephant.

It is against the rules for the elephants to use their trunks to

12 ______________________________ the ball.

A total of **13** ______________________________ elephants are required for a game to take place.

The participants are in action for a total of **14** ______________________________ during each game.

The stick used in the game is both **15** ____________ and ____________ .

The elephants sometimes want to **16** ______________________________ in front of a goal.

An elephant with a bad **17** ______________________________ will be taken out of a game.

African elephants are not used because **18** ______________________________ cause a problem.

You will hear five different people talking about cities they have visited. For questions 19–23, choose from the list (A–H) the opinion each person gives about the city. Use the letters only once. There are three extra letters which you do not need to use.

A   It was exactly as I had imagined.

Speaker 1   **19**

B   It is not as good as it used to be.

Speaker 2   **20**

C   It is smaller than I had thought.

Speaker 3   **21**

D   It is hard to find your way around it.

Speaker 4   **22**

E   It is overrated.

Speaker 5   **23**

F   It is better for a long visit than a short one.

G   It can get too crowded.

H   It was even better than I expected.

PART 4

You will hear an interview with someone who is involved in the music business. For questions 24–30, choose the best answer (A, B or C).

---

24 What does James say about the radio station he started?
   A Its name was very appropriate.
   B It was more popular than he had expected.
   C It was not very expensive to run.

24

25 What does James say about people's attitudes towards his age?
   A They were nicer to him when he was 12 than when he was 16.
   B They were more jealous of him when he was 12 than when he was 16.
   C They expected more of him when he was 16 than when he was 12.

25

26 James says that his career in music has included
   A taking over a local radio station.
   B making advertisements.
   C setting up new festivals.

26

27 What do we learn about advertising on James' TV channel?
   A There isn't any of it.
   B It always includes music.
   C It doesn't interrupt the programmes.

27

28 What does James say about the people interviewed on the channel?
   A They have to say something interesting.
   B They enjoy being interviewed.
   C They often say unexpected things.

28

29 What does James say about his ideas?
   A Some of them are not very realistic.
   B He expects to have good ones all the time.
   C He makes sure that he doesn't forget them.

29

30 James's advice to listeners who might want to go into business is to
   A forget about past problems.
   B learn from past mistakes.
   C take big risks.

30

Speaking (14 minutes)

PART 1 (2 minutes)

Where you live

- Where do you live?
- How long have you been living there?
- What kind of building do you live in?
- What do you like / dislike about the town / village / district where you live?

Travel

- Have you been to many other countries? ..... (Which ones?)
- Would you like to travel more? ..... (Where?)
- What's the best country / city / region that you've visited? ..... (Why?)
- Which country / city / region would you most like to visit? ..... (Why?)

School

- What is / was your favourite school subject? ...... (Why?)
- Describe one of your school friends.
- Which school subject(s) do / did you most dislike? ...... (Why?)
- Describe a teacher at your school.

PART 2 (4 minutes)

1 **Outdoor activities**
2 **People's rooms**

Candidate A	Look at the two photographs 1A and 1B on page 24. They show people doing outdoor activities. Compare the photographs and say what the people are trying to do. *Candidate A talks on his / her own for about 1 minute.*
Candidate B	Which of the activities would you prefer to do, and why? *Candidate B talks on his / her own for about 30 seconds.*
Candidate B	Look at the two photographs 2A and 2B on page 24. They show people's rooms. Compare the photographs and say whose rooms they might be. *Candidate B talks on his / her own for about 1 minute.*
Candidate A	Which of the rooms is most similar to yours, and in what ways? *Candidate A talks on his / her own for about 30 seconds.*

- What are the people trying to do?

1A

1B

- Whose rooms do you think these are?

2A

2B

Exhibitions for a museum

PART 3 (4 minutes)

Imagine that a local museum is trying to increase visitor numbers. Look at the ideas for new exhibitions that are being considered by the museum.

First, talk to each other about how popular each of the suggestions would be.

Then decide which two would attract the most visitors to the museum.

Candidates A and B discuss this together for about 3 minutes.

PART 4 (4 minutes)

- Do you like going to museums or art galleries? ..... (Why / Why not?)
- Which of the subjects interests you the most and which interests you the least? ..... (Why?)
- What are the most well-known museums or art galleries in the place you come from? What do they have in them?
- What kind of things do museums offer to attract young people?
- What is the most interesting museum or art gallery that you've been to? ...... (Why?)
- Which museum or art gallery would you most like to visit? Where is it? What does it have in it? What would you like to see there? ..... (Why?)
- Some people think that museums and art galleries are boring. Do you agree?

Reading and Use of English (1 hour 15 minutes)

<u>PART 1</u>

For questions 1–8, read the text below and decide which answer (A, B, C or D) best fits each gap. There is an example at the beginning (0).

Mark your answers on the separate answer sheet.

Example:

0 **A** estimated   **B** awaited   **C** assessed   **D** predicted

0	A	B	C	D

Britain's first shopping centre

When Brent Cross Shopping Centre in London opened it was the first large-scale indoor shopping centre in Britain and many people **0**_________ it would be a **1**_________ failure. Instead, the centre, with its 75 stores, started a shopping **2**_________ in Britain.

'They said it **3**_________ no chance of becoming popular, but in the first week it was packed, and that's how it's **4**_________ on,' said George Dorman, who has been working as a fruit and vegetable sales assistant at the Waitrose store since it opened. It's a **5**_________ achievement and 'I've enjoyed every **6**_________ minute of it,' he said.

Sisters Jeanette Harris and Lydia Neidus have both been working as sales assistants at the Fenwicks store since the centre opened. Ms Neidus said: 'The more you get involved, the more you love it because you've seen everything and you've **7**_________ so much knowledge about it all.' Her sister added: 'I **8**_________ as if it was just yesterday when I started and I've loved every minute.'

1	**A** whole	**B** complete	**C** full	**D** true
2	**A** novelty	**B** alteration	**C** conversion	**D** revolution
3	**A** took	**B** stood	**C** ran	**D** held
4	**A** stayed	**B** carried	**C** moved	**D** stuck
5	**A** great	**B** high	**C** large	**D** vast
6	**A** actual	**B** single	**C** individual	**D** separate
7	**A** increased	**B** gained	**C** raised	**D** expanded
8	**A** feel	**B** seem	**C** sense	**D** find

PART 2

For questions **9–16,** *read the text below and think of the word which best fits each gap. Use only* **one** *word in each gap. There is an example at the beginning (**0**).*

Write your answers **IN CAPITAL LETTERS on the separate answer sheet.**

Example:

| **0** | H | O | W | | | | | | | | | |

See dinosaurs eating!

Dinosaurs died out more than 60 million years ago, so **0** __________ can we tell what they used to eat? Find out at the Cameron Museum, where you can step **9** __________ in time and join some dinosaurs enjoying their lunch. **10** __________ you enter the new Meet the Dinosaurs exhibition, you'll meet four full-size dinosaur heads, each of them munching away on their favourite food. The model dinosaurs are **11** __________ realistic that you could easily forget that they're not real.

Scientists have pieced **12** __________ information from fossils to work out that dinosaurs with large claws and sharp teeth ate meat, while flatter teeth were used **13** __________ grinding plants. So Tyrannosaurus rex, with its prehistoric table manners **14** __________ teeth as sharp as razors, might not have been the **15** __________ relaxing dinner guest!

But, whether you're a meat eater or a vegetarian, **16** __________ not come along to the exhibition and make sure you don't miss an incredible day out!

PART 3

For questions 17–24, read the text below. Use the word given in capitals at the end of some of the lines to form a word that fits in the gap in the same line. There is an example at the beginning (0).

Write your answers IN CAPITAL LETTERS on the separate answer sheet.

Example:

ESCORTED TOURS

Organizing a holiday can be a very **0** ___________ task. Some people find   **CHALLENGE**

the experience as **17** ___________ as the daily demands of work and family   **STRESS**

commitments. If you are in this situation, you may find that taking an

escorted holiday is the ideal **18** ___________ .   **SOLVE**

    Escorted holidays offer a great balance between sightseeing, entertainment

and leisure time, with the added advantage that you have the services of a

professional tour manager, who **19** ___________ you throughout the trip,   **COMPANY**

acting as your **20** ___________ guide. From the first day to the last, tour   **PERSON**

managers make your holiday experience even more **21** ___________ because   **MEMORY**

of the invaluable information and **22** ___________ suggestions they provide.   **HELP**

Your tour manager will give you many **23** ___________ into the place you are   **SIGHT**

visiting, including useful information on the distinctive characteristics

of the place, such as regional food and local entertainment.

    If you book one of the escorted holiday packages that we offer, you can be

sure that you will have a **24** ___________ authentic travel experience.   **TRUE**

PART 4

For questions 25–30, complete the second sentence so that it has a similar meaning to the first sentence, using the word given. Do not change the word given. *You must use between two and five words, including the word given. Here is an example (0).*

Example:

0 Making new friends was easy for her.

DIFFICULT

She didn't _________________ new friends.

The gap can be filled with the words 'find it difficult to make', so you write:

0	FIND IT DIFFICULT TO MAKE

Write only the missing words IN CAPITAL LETTERS on the separate answer sheet.

___

25 He didn't buy a present for her, he gave her some money.

INSTEAD

He gave her some money _________________ present.

26 A temporary manager is running the shop at the moment.

RUN

The shop _________________ a temporary manager at the moment.

27 How long is your journey from home to work?

TAKE

How long _________________ get from home to work?

28 When I rang the box office, the tickets had all been sold.

LEFT

There _________________ when I rang the box office.

29 If public opinion doesn't change suddenly, he'll win the next election.

SUDDEN

Unless _________________ change in public opinion, he'll win the next election.

30 This is the happiest that Paula has ever been.

HAPPIER

Paula _________________ she is now.

You are going to read an extract from a novel. For questions 31–36, choose the answer (A, B, C or D) which you think fits best according to the text.

Mark your answers on the separate answer sheet.

The Fulton Chain Floating Library is only a tiny room, a closet really, below decks in Charlie Eckler's pickle boat. It is nothing like the proper library they have in Old Forge, but it has its own element of surprise. Mr Eckler uses the room to store his wares, and when he finally gets around to moving a chest of tea or a sack of cornmeal, you never know what you might find. And once in a while, the main library in Herkimer sends up a new book or two. It's nice to get your hands on a new book before everyone else does. While the pages are still clean and white and the spine hasn't been snapped.

I stepped onto the boat and went below decks. The *House of Mirth* was under *W*, like Mr Eckler said it would be, only it was wedged next to *Mrs Wiggs of the Cabbage Patch*. Mr Eckler sometimes gets authors and titles confused. I signed it out in a ledger he kept on top of a molasses barrel, then rooted around behind a crate of eggs, a jar of marbles and a box of dried dates but found nothing I hadn't already read. I remembered to get the bag of cornmeal we needed. I wished I could buy oatmeal or white flour instead, but cornmeal cost less and went further. I was to get a ten-pound bag. The fifty-pound bag cost more to buy but was cheaper per pound and I'd told Pa so, but he said only rich people can afford to be thrifty.

Just as I was about to climb back upstairs, something caught my eye – a box of composition books. Real pretty ones with hard covers on them, and swirly paint designs, and a ribbon to mark your place. I put the cornmeal down, and Mrs Wharton too, and picked one up. Its pages were smooth and white. I thought it would be a fine thing to write on paper that nice. The pages in my old composition book were rough and had blurry blue lines printed on them, and were made with so little care that there were slivers of wood visible in them.

I handed Mr Eckler fifty cents of my father's money for the cornmeal. 'How much is this?' I asked, holding up one of the pretty composition books. I had sixty cents from all the fiddleheads Weaver and I had sold to the Eagle Bay Hotel.

It was money I knew I should have given to my pa. I'd meant to, really. I just hadn't gotten around to it.

'Those notebooks? They're expensive, Mattie. Italians made them. I've got to get forty-five cents apiece,' he said. 'I've got some others coming in for fifteen cents in a week or so if you can wait.'

Forty-five cents was a good deal of money, but I didn't want the ones for fifteen cents, not after I'd seen the others. I had ideas. Tons of them. For stories and poems. I chewed the inside of my cheek, deliberating. I knew I would have to write a lot when I went to Barnard College– *if* I went to Barnard College – and it might be a good idea to get a head start. Weaver had said I should be using my words, not just collecting them, and I knew they would just glide across this beautiful paper, and when I was done writing them, I could close them safely inside the covers. Just like a real book. Guilt gnawed at my insides. I took the money from my pocket and gave it to Mr Eckler quickly, so the thing was done and I couldn't change my mind.

31 What does Mattie say about the library in Mr Eckler's boat?
   A New books are frequently added to it.
   B All the books in it are in excellent condition.
   C It contains books that are hidden from view.
   D Mr Eckler doesn't know exactly what is in it.

32 When Mattie found the new book, she
   A discovered that there were other new books nearby.
   B saw that it had been put in the wrong place.
   C followed Mr Eckler's system for borrowing books.
   D had to move something so that she could find it.

33 What was the situation concerning the cornmeal?
   A Her father was unable to save money by buying the bigger bag.
   B Her father could not see the point of buying the bigger bag.
   C Her father felt that cornmeal was better than oatmeal or white flour.
   D Her father had decided to stop buying what he usually bought.

34 One reason why Mattie liked the look of the composition books was that
   A the covers were shiny.
   B the pages were completely clear.
   C the pages were thicker than in her old book.
   D they had better ribbons than her old book.

35 When Mattie asked Mr Eckler how much the composition books cost, he said that
   A they weren't really worth the money.
   B they were not the books he had been expecting to receive.
   C he did not expect many people to buy them.
   D he had no choice about how much to charge for them.

36 While she was buying one of the books, Mattie thought about
   A how she could use it for making lists of words.
   B what the experience of writing in it would be like.
   C what people at Barnard College would think of it.
   D whether she would have enough ideas to fill the whole book.

You are going to read an article about an activity in Spain. Six sentences have been removed from the article. Choose from the sentences A–G the one which fits each gap (37–42). There is one extra sentence which you do not need to use.

Mark your answers on the separate answer sheet.

The Tower and the Glory

Chris Wilson starts at the bottom when he joins a Spanish team making competitive human pyramids

A large man jams his foot in my ear and jumps on to my shoulders. He is quickly followed by another only slightly smaller gentleman who grabs my belt and shimmies up me like a pole. Another follows. My face contorts with pain as the fourth tier mounts on to my back and I begin to sway dangerously. **37**____________.

'Castelling' (making human castles) is a family sport in Catalonia. Groups normally consist of everyone from tiny children, through awkward adolescents and wiry women, to well-built men at the bottom. **38**____________ I had also heard that being overweight and unfit would not count against me. Sure enough, when I turned up for my first training session, I could sense that, for the first time in years, my ever-expanding physique was being appreciatively looked at.

Castelling began almost 200 years ago near Tarragona, just south of Barcelona. Out of nowhere, it seems that people suddenly began forming themselves into human towers. Since then the sport, if you can call it that, has become an expression

of Catalan identity, with groups competing to build ever higher and more elegant structures.

39____________ Once or twice it has managed a six-tier tower. The top teams regularly manage eight or nine. It was my intention to add a little British beef to the group to help them reach the next level in time for the competitions to be held tomorrow in Barcelona on the National Day of Catalonia.

At first I had thought that I might like to go on top to bask in the glory, but the club's president soon put me straight. He indicated a spindly little girl who looked as though she had been raised entirely on broccoli, and not much of it at that. It is she who has pride of place on top of the pyramid. **40**____________ For my first try-out I was given the role of *segones mans* (second hands), which meant that I supported the wrists of the man who supported the buttocks of the first rank of the pyramid.

Once I had assumed my position, people began to scramble up me and on to the tower without warning. **41**____________ Still, my hard work must have been appreciated because I was quickly promoted to be *primeres mans* and support the bottoms of the first level of the pyramid that we were making under the watchful eye of the artistic director.

My performance in the 'hands' section had obviously been satisfactory because at the third training session I was called forward and given the very great honour of the President's Belt. **42**____________ Being offered this belt, still warm from the very waist of the President, was a clear gesture that me and my bulk had been accepted. Finally, I had made it to the bottom of the pile.

A The best I could hope for was to be at the bottom, but even that honour has to be earned.

B So I knew that everyone at the training session that night would have cheered with good-natured delight if I had done that.

C I had been attracted to castelling because I had been told that it requires almost no skill or co-ordination.

D Within seconds I had assisted in the formation of a three-tier tower without really noticing what was happening.

E It's not easy being the bottom man of a human pyramid.

F Each casteller is wound into a large strip of material worn around the waist to support the back and to help the other castellers grip when they climb.

G The group I had joined in Figueres, near the French border, is very much a second-division outfit.

You are going to read a magazine article about the history of the bicycle. For questions 43–52, choose from the sections of the article (A–D). The sections may be chosen more than once.

Mark your answers on the separate answer sheet.

In which section of the article are the following mentioned?

features that were not added because they were considered problematic	**43**
a design that is exactly the same as that of current products	**44**
a product that became popular despite its price in comparison with an existing product	**45**
a warning that affected the appeal of a certain product	**46**
an attempt to get publicity	**47**
the possibility of injury because of where the rider sat	**48**
products that were introduced to compensate for a disadvantage of another product	**49**
a design that some manufacturers felt would not become popular	**50**
people riding a certain product in order to impress others	**51**
the motivation of one set of people for changing bicycle design	**52**

Wheels that changed the world

A The bicycle was an absolutely extraordinary creation. Inventors had first begun to wrestle with the challenge of coming up with a human-powered vehicle in the 17th century. The beginnings of the modern bicycle emerged in 1818 when Karl von Drais, an eccentric German baron, invented what we now know as the hobbyhorse. It was bicycle-shaped with wooden wheels but had no pedals: the rider had to push it forward with his feet. The hobbyhorse could be afforded only by true gentlemen, and it soon became a much sought-after status symbol. But the craze died out after a year following a statement from the London College of Surgeons, which said darkly that the hobbyhorse could cause 'internal injuries'.

B Brilliant minds continued to wrestle with the mechanical horse but made slow progress. Even Britain's top engineer, Isambard Kingdom Brunel, could come up with nothing better than a hobbyhorse that ran on railway tracks. Finally, in 1887, a Parisian blacksmith called Pierre Michaux added a pair of pedals to a hobbyhorse, and the bicycle was born. The Michaux bicycle had pedals fixed directly to the front wheel, just like a child's tricycle today. Made largely of iron, it weighed as much as a fridge but was easy to ride and took a man up to five miles with the effort he would use to walk only one. Michaux's first newspaper advertisement in May 1867 offered 'pedal velocipedes' for 250 francs. At this price only the wealthy could afford one and a group of 20 young men spent their days showing off their 'steeds' before fascinated crowds in the Bois de Boulogne. Michaux was soon producing 20 bicycles a day, and decided to organize a women's race as a stunt to boost his sales further. Within a year, there were 50,000 bicycles in France.

C Not to be outdone by their French counterparts, British engineers set about improving bicycle design with wire-spoked wheels and solid rubber tyres. Gears and chains were still thought too heavy and complex to be fitted to a bicycle, so designers could increase top speed only by increasing the size of the front wheel. Eventually front wheels grew until they were 5ft and the penny farthing was born. Speeds of 20 mph were now possible, but the rider's seat was directly above the front wheel, which made riding in a skirt impossible, so women were effectively barred from bicycles. To make up for it, manufacturers developed tricycles with low seats. The penny farthing's biggest drawback was its danger: the high seat was difficult to climb into, and once up there the driver had a long way to fall.

D In 1885, John Starley launched the Rover Safety Bicycle, the first model to adopt what we now think of as the traditional design. The bicycle industry was unimpressed, as it had a chain-driven rear wheel, which added weight, and a low seat, which made male riders look a bit ridiculous. But it turned out to be faster than a penny farthing because it was more aerodynamic. More importantly, the Rover could be ridden in a skirt. It was more expensive than a penny farthing, but its practicality was just what the public wanted. Soon there were half a million bicycles in the UK. Between 1890 and 1900, the bicycle was refined until the basic design became very similar to the featherweights that modern champions ride in the Tour de France. Lightweight steel tubing, the diamond-shaped frame, gears and pneumatic tyres with separate inner tubes all became common. Top speeds of 25 mph could now be reached. At last the cyclist could outrun a galloping horse.

Writing (1 hour 20 minutes)

PART 1

*You **must** answer this question. Write your answer in 140–190 words in an appropriate style.*

1   In your English class you have been talking about The News on television and in other media.
    Now, your English teacher has asked you to write an essay.
    Write an essay using **all** the notes and give reasons for your point of view.

> What kind of news in the media has the most influence on people?
>
> **Notes**
> Write about:
> 1.   politics
> 2.   crime
> 3.   ___________________ (your own idea)

Write an answer to **one** *of the questions* **2–4** *in this part. Write your answer in* **140–190** *words in an appropriate style.*

2   You recently saw this notice in an international magazine.

LOCAL REPORTERS WANTED!

We're looking for people to send us reports on what has been happening in their village, city or region over the past year. You can tell us about important events, ordinary day-to-day life, people in general or specific individuals.

We'll publish some of the reports in a special section.

Write your **report**.

3   You have seen the following announcement on an international student website.

ARE YOU A MEMBER OF A CLUB? TELL US ABOUT IT.

Write an article about a club that you are a member of.

Why do you like being a member of it?

We'll put the best articles in a special section on the website.

Write your **article**.

4   You have seen this announcement in an English-language magazine.

FANCY YOURSELF AS AN INTERVIEWER?

Is there someone that you'd like to interview? It doesn't have to be a living person. Write and tell us who you'd like to interview if you had the chance. Why would you like to interview that person? What would you ask?

We'll publish the best letters in the next issue.

Write your **letter**.

Listening (40 minutes)

PART 1

You will hear people talking in eight different situations. For questions 1–8, choose the best answer (A, B or C).

---

1 You hear part of an interview with a sportsman.
What does he say about playing for the national team?

   A He doesn't think it will happen soon.

   B It isn't his main concern at the moment.   **1**

   C The possibility of it happening has put him under pressure.

2 You hear the introduction to a radio programme.
What is the speaker doing?

   A contrasting weather forecasting in the past and the present

   B explaining why weather forecasting has become more accurate   **2**

   C joking about how people used to forecast the weather

3 You hear a man talking about reading aloud to children.
What opinion does he express?

   A Short stories are better than longer books.

   B The choice of book may not be important.   **3**

   C It's hard to know what will make children laugh.

4 You hear someone talking about work.
What is his situation?

   A He has just left a job.

   B He is thinking of leaving his job.   **4**

   C He has just started a new job.

5 You hear someone talking about his childhood.
   What does he mention?

   A a habit he regards as strange

   B regret about some of his behaviour

   C how much he has changed

6 You hear someone talking about something that happened at a party.
   How did the speaker feel?

   A upset

   B amused

   C frightened

7 You hear part of a talk about blues music.
   What is the speaker talking about?

   A why it originated in a certain area

   B how popular it was in the past compared with today

   C its importance in the history of popular music

8 You hear someone on the radio talking about a website for consumers.
   What is the speaker's purpose?

   A to encourage consumers to make complaints

   B to inform consumers about a source of information

   C to describe common problems for consumers

PART 2

You will hear a radio reporter talking about indoor skydiving. For questions 9–18, complete the sentences with a word or short phrase.

INDOOR SKYDIVING

The fans in the tunnel are normally used for putting air into **9** _________________________ .

It has been said that the machine works like a huge **10** _________________________ .

The walls in the tunnel are made of **11** _________________________ .

The only parts of the body that can get hurt in the tunnel are the

12 _____________ and _____________ .

You have to be **13** _________________________ years old to use the tunnel.

You have to wear **14** _________________________ when you use the tunnel.

Beginners have two **15** _________________________ lessons in the tunnel with an

instructor.

During lessons, you get into a position as if you have a **16** _________________________

in your hands.

The person who created the wind tunnel refers to it as a **17** '_________________________'.

Indoor skydiving has become a sport called **18** _________________________ .

PART 3

You will hear five different people talking about the reasons why they became very successful. For questions 19–23, choose from the list (A–H) the reason each person gives for their success. Use the letters only once. There are three extra letters which you do not need to use.

A   natural ability

Speaker 1   **19**

B   lessons learnt from making mistakes

Speaker 2   **20**

C   encouragement from others

Speaker 3   **21**

D   careful planning

Speaker 4   **22**

E   constant good luck

Speaker 5   **23**

F   determination to improve

G   good advice from others

H   lack of competition

You will hear part of a radio interview with a woman called Tania Wade about taking up running as a regular activity. For questions 24–30, choose the best answer (A, B or C).

24 Tania says that when she was younger,

    A she envied people who did a lot of physical activity.
    B she knew that she ought to take up some kind of physical activity.
    C she hated the idea of doing any kind of physical activity.

`24`

25 Tania says that if people take up running,

    A she can guarantee that there will be certain benefits.
    B they will wonder why they didn't do it before.
    C it will become a long-term interest for them.

`25`

26 Tania says that, in comparison with other activities and sports, running is

    A more enjoyable.
    B more convenient.
    C more beneficial.

`26`

27 What does Tania say about people who feel that they can't take up running?

    A They should talk to people who do run.
    B They may be right.
    C They know that their attitude is wrong.

`27`

28 Tania warns people who take up running not to

    A be competitive.
    B give up as soon as there is a problem.
    C ignore pain.

`28`

29 What advice does Tania give about running technique?

    A Change the position of your arms from time to time.
    B Think of your arms as if they were parts of an engine.
    C Pay more attention to your arms than any other part of your body.

`29`

30 What does Tania say about breathing while running?

    A Some bad advice is sometimes given about it.
    B It takes some time to develop the best technique for it.
    C There isn't a correct or incorrect way of doing it.

`30`

Speaking (14 minutes)

PART 1 (2 minutes)

Family and friends

- Describe briefly the members of your family.
- What kind of things do you talk about with your friends?
- What influence have your family and friends had on you?
- What interests do your family and friends have?

Money and possessions

- What would you buy if you suddenly had a lot of money? ..... (Why?)
- Do you want to be richer than you are now? ..... (Why? / Why not?)
- What do people of your age generally want to buy? ..... (Why?)
- What are your favourite possessions? ..... (Why?)

Food and cooking

- What do you usually have for breakfast?
- What is your favourite evening meal?
- What dish(es) are you good at cooking?
- Do you have a healthy diet?

PART 2 (4 minutes)

1 Films
2 Cooking

Candidate A	Look at the two photographs 1A and 1B on page 44. They show adverts for films.
	Compare the photographs and say what the characteristics of each kind of film are.
	Candidate A talks on his / her own for about 1 minute.
Candidate B	Which of the films would you prefer to see, and why?
	Candidate B talks on his / her own for about 30 seconds.
Candidate B	Look at the two photographs 2A and 2B on page 44. They show people cooking meals.
	Compare the photographs and say what you think the situation is in each photograph.
	Candidate B talks on his / her own for about 1 minute.
Candidate A	Which of the people cooking would you prefer to be, and why?
	Candidate A talks on his / her own for about 30 seconds.

■ What are the characteristics of each kind of film?

1A

1B

■ What do you think the situation is?

2A

2B

TEST 2

'Special day' prize

PART 3 (4 minutes)

Imagine that you are organizing a competition at the place where you work or study. The prize for the winner is going to be a special day and you have to choose what kind of special day the prize will be. Look at the special days offered by a company in their brochure.

First, talk to each other about how attractive each of the possible prizes would be.

Then decide which one should be the prize.

Candidates A and B discuss this together for about 3 minutes.

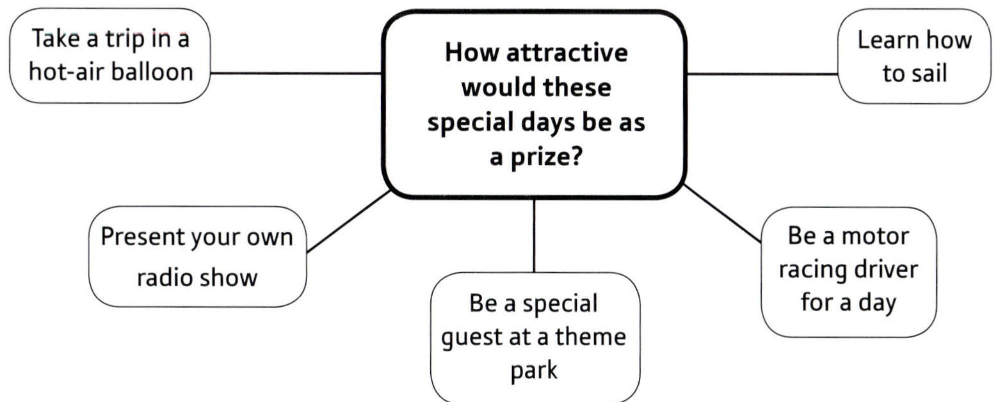

PART 4 (4 minutes)

- Which of the special days would you like to experience personally? ..... (Why?)
- Which of the special days would you definitely not want to take part in? ...... (Why?)
- What dangerous sports are popular in your country?
- What makes people want to take part in dangerous sports?
- Why do people like going to theme parks? Which ones are good and which ones are not, in your opinion?
- Some people say that young people don't have a wide range of interests. Do you agree?

Reading and Use of English (1 hour 15 minutes)

<u>PART 1</u>

For questions 1–8, read the text below and decide which answer (A, B, C or D) best fits each gap. There is an example at the beginning (0).

Mark your answers on the separate answer sheet.

Example:

0   A convince   **B** guess   **C** believe   **D** value

0	A	B	C	D
	—	—	**—**	—

Neighbours influence buying decisions

However objective we **0** ___________ ourselves to be, most of us do not judge a product solely on its merits, considering quality, value and style before making a decision. **1** ___________ , we are easily influenced by the people around us. There is nothing **2** ___________ with this. It is probably a smarter way to make decisions than **3** ___________ on only our own opinions.

   Research in Finland recently found overwhelming evidence that neighbours have a big influence on buying decisions. When one of a person's ten nearest neighbours bought a car, the **4** ___________ that that person would buy a car of the same brand during the next week and a half **5** ___________ by 86 per cent. The researchers argued that it was not just a **6** ___________ of envy. Used cars seemed to attract neighbours even more than new cars. This suggested that people were not trying to **7** ___________ up with their neighbours, they were keen to learn from them. Since used cars are less reliable, a recommendation of one can **8** ___________ influence a buying decision.

1	**A** What's more	**B** Instead	**C** Unlike	**D** In place
2	**A** wrong	**B** silly	**C** bad	**D** daft
3	**A** basing	**B** trusting	**C** supposing	**D** relying
4	**A** chances	**B** potential	**C** possibilities	**D** forecast
5	**A** boosted	**B** rose	**C** enlarged	**D** lifted
6	**A** thing	**B** point	**C** matter	**D** fact
7	**A** keep	**B** stay	**C** hold	**D** follow
8	**A** fiercely	**B** strongly	**C** firmly	**D** intensely

*For questions **9–16**, read the text below and think of the word which best fits each gap. Use only **one** word in each gap. There is an example at the beginning (**0**).*

*Write your answers **IN CAPITAL LETTERS** on the separate answer sheet.*

Example:

| **0** | S | O | M | E | T | H | I | N | G | | | | |

Learning a musical instrument

Learning to play an instrument is **0**__________ that can give a lot of pleasure. It's also an achievement and a skill **9**__________ stays with you for life. Music has a part to play in everyone's life, and has been described **10**__________ a 'primary language'.

A lot of adults regret not **11**__________ learnt to play an instrument when they were younger. But it is never **12**__________ late to learn! And the advantages of learning an instrument are far greater than just the pleasure of producing a marvellous sound. When you've progressed far **13**__________, there are lots of amateur groups which you can join **14**__________ you want to be part of a larger group. Once you've reached a good enough standard to join a band or orchestra, you add the team skills like **15**__________ you get from playing sport. There's also a great social side to playing with others, as **16**__________ as the chance to travel through touring.

For questions 17–24, read the text below. Use the word given in capitals at the end of some of the lines to form a word that fits in the gap in the same line. There is an example at the beginning (0).

Write your answers IN CAPITAL LETTERS on the separate answer sheet.

Example:

| 0 | F | R | I | E | N | D | L | Y | | | | | |

THE COUPLES WITH IDENTICAL LIVES

When Frank and Vera Jackson met a **0** __________ couple on holiday   **FRIEND**

in Spain also called Frank and Vera (but with a different

surname: Bentley), at first they must have laughed at the **17** __________ .   **COINCIDE**

But when they got into **18** __________ with their namesakes, they made   **CONVERSE**

some surprising **19** __________ and realized that they had much more in   **DISCOVER**

common.

    Both couples had had their **20** __________ on the same date in the   **WED**

same year and at the same time. Both couples each had two daughters, with

dates of **21** __________ in the same years, and six grandchildren. Mr Jackson   **BORN**

worked in the car industry in Oxford; Mr Bentley had done **22** __________   **EXACT**

the same job but in Dagenham. Their wives, who had both worked for the

same bank, had both lost their **23** __________ rings and were wearing   **ENGAGE**

identical gold watches. 'I'm sure people everywhere lead identical

lives,' said Mr Jackson, 'but to meet our doubles was **24** __________ .'   **BELIEVE**

For questions 25–30, complete the second sentence so that it has a similar meaning to the first sentence, using the word given. **Do not change the word given.** *You must use between* **two** *and* **five** *words, including the word given. Here is an example (* **0** *).*

Example:

0 Making new friends was easy for her.

DIFFICULT

She didn't ________________________ new friends.

The gap can be filled with the words 'find it difficult to make', so you write:

0	F I N D I T D I F F I C U L T T O M A K E

Write **only** *the missing words* **IN CAPITAL LETTERS on the separate answer sheet.**

---

25 Her behaviour tends to be bad when she is under pressure.

TENDENCY

She ________________________ badly when she is under pressure.

26 My brother earns half of what I earn.

TWICE

I earn ________________________ my brother.

27 I got angry because of the assistant's attitude.

MADE

The assistant's attitude ________________________ temper.

28 He plays so skilfully that nobody can beat him.

MUCH

He plays with ________________________ that nobody can beat him.

29 They were late because they got stuck in traffic.

RESULT

They were late ________________________ stuck in traffic.

30 Yesterday I met one of my friends by chance in the supermarket.

RAN

Yesterday I ________________ ____________ mine in the supermarket.

You are going to read a newspaper article about careers advice. For questions 31–36, choose the answer (A, B, C or D) which you think fits best according to the text.

Mark your answers on the separate answer sheet.

Finding the career that fits your personality

'If you've finished your exams and have absolutely no idea what to do next, you're not alone,' says Sheridan Hughes, an occupational psychologist at Career Analysts, a career counselling service. 'At 18, it can be very difficult to know what you want to do because you don't really know what you're interested in.' Careers guidance, adds Alexis Hallam, one of her colleagues, is generally poor and 'people can end up in the wrong job and stay there for years because they're good at something without actually enjoying it.'

To discover what people are good at, and more fundamentally, what they will enjoy doing, Career Analysts give their clients a battery of personality profile questionnaires and psychometric tests. An in-depth interview follows, in which the test results are discussed and different career paths and options are explored with the aid of an occupational psychologist. Career Analysts offers guidance to everyone, from teenagers to retirees looking for a new focus in life. The service sounded just what I needed. Dividing my time as I do between teaching and freelance journalism, I definitely need advice about consolidating my career. Being too ancient for Career Analysts' student career option guidance and not, unfortunately, at the executive level yet, I opted for the career management package.

This is aimed at people who are established in their jobs and who either want a change or some advice about planning the next step in their careers.

Having filled in a multitude of personality indicator questionnaires at home, I then spent a rather gruelling morning being aptitude-tested at Career Analysts' offices. The tests consisted of logical reasoning followed by verbal, mechanical and spatial aptitude papers. Logical reasoning required me to pick out the next shape in a sequence of triangles, squares and oblongs. I tried my best but knew that it was really a lost cause. I fared rather better when it came to verbal aptitude – finding the odd one out in a series of words couldn't be simpler. My complacency was short-lived, however, when I was confronted with images of levers and pulleys for the mechanical aptitude papers. My mind went blank. I had no idea what would happen to wheel X when string Y was pulled.

Having completed my personality and aptitude tests, I sat down with Sheridan Hughes, who asked me fairly searching personal and professional questions. What do my parents and siblings do for a living? Why had I chosen to do an English degree? 'I need to get a picture of you as a person and how you've come to be who you are,' she explained. 'What we do works because it's a mixture of science and counselling. We use objective psychometric measures to discover our clients' natural strengths and abilities and then we talk to them about what they want from life.'

There were no real surprises in my own test results, nor in the interview that followed it. 'We're interested in patterns,' Mrs Hughes explained, 'and the pattern for you is strongly verbal and communicative.' This was putting it rather kindly. I had come out as average on the verbal skills test and below average in logic, numerical, perceptual and mechanical reasoning. My spatial visualization was so bad it was almost off the scale. 'A career in cartography, navigation, tiling or architecture would not be playing to your strengths,' she said delicately.

Mrs Hughes encouraged me to expand the writing side of my career and gave me straightforward, practical suggestions as to how I could go about it. 'Widen the scope of your articles,' she said. 'You could develop an interest in medical and psychological fields.' These latter, she said, would sit comfortably with an interest in human behaviour indicated on my personality-profiling questionnaires. She suggested that I consider writing e-learning content for on-line courses, an avenue that would never have occurred to me.

31 Which of the following is mentioned in the first paragraph?

   A people underestimating their own abilities
   B people accepting inappropriate advice
   C people being unwilling to take risks
   D people constantly changing their minds

32 What does the writer say about Career Analysts in the second paragraph?

   A It is about to offer a service for people at executive level.
   B The range of services it offers is unique.
   C She was initially doubtful that it could be useful to her.
   D Only one of its services was relevant to her.

33 What happened when the writer took the aptitude tests?

   A She found two of the papers extremely difficult.
   B She put in very little effort on any of them.
   C She didn't understand what she was required to do on one of them.
   D The papers were not what she had been expecting.

34 Some of the questions Sheridan Hughes asked concerned the writer's

   A opinions of the tests and questionnaires.
   B relationships with family members.
   C main regrets.
   D progress through life.

35 The writer felt that during the interview, Mrs Hughes

   A was keen not to upset her concerning her test results.
   B seemed surprised at how badly she had done in the tests.
   C was being honest about her strengths and weaknesses.
   D preferred to avoid talking about her test results.

36 The advice Mrs Hughes gave to the writer included the suggestion that she should

   A think about taking a course on writing.
   B concentrate only on writing and not on any other kind of work.
   C increase the number of subjects she writes about.
   D do something she had previously considered unappealing.

You are going to read an article about martial arts. Six sentences have been removed from the article. Choose from the sentences A–G the one which fits each gap (37–42). There is one extra sentence which you do not need to use.

Mark your answers on the separate answer sheet.

Martial Arts Classes

Learn an effective fighting and self-defence system

Tony Chang is a martial artist who has served a long apprenticeship in both the internal and external arts. He is respected worldwide as a martial arts instructor in kenpo, t'ai chi ch'uan and chi kung and runs several of his own clubs in Manchester. He also has several training videos and DVDs to his credit. In fact, he was one of the pioneers of teaching the Martial Arts Techniques series on the worldwide web. **37** _____________

Tony is now in the process of producing what he considers to be the 'ultimate street survival' DVD, combining fighting and self-defence with energy (chi) development and enhancement. A few years ago, he was inducted into the Martial Arts Hall of Fame for integrating his internal martial arts knowledge with the fast-paced external striking style that kenpo is noted for, and developing kenpo taiji. **38** _____________

It is not based purely on physical strength.
39 _____________ As Tony explains, 'It is 50 per cent physical and 50 per cent in the mind. It is a scientific fact that we have three brains inside our head. As well as the intellectual brain which forms 90 per cent of our overall brain, five per cent is the artistic brain which is responsible for subconscious body movement and five per cent constitutes the reptilian brain, which is purely reflex. This is the same brain as that of all reptiles, such as snakes and crocodiles – this is our survival brain.'

40 _____________ That is because they use the logical, intellectual brain to teach logical pre-arranged techniques. However, fighting is totally illogical and we cannot apply logic to an illogical situation, so our response to an attack must be reflex. Students achieve this in kenpo taiji by learning how to access their reptilian brain. Tony says there is no time to think in a fight situation. 'If you stop to think, you'll get hit,' he explains.

Tony is running beginners' classes in kenpo taiji.
41 _____________ These include how to adopt certain body postures which encourage energy to flow from an energy storage centre known as the *dan tien* up to the brain stem. Students are then in reptile brain mode, ready to defend themselves against any attacker. And they learn training methods designed by the ancient Chinese masters to programme this part of the brain subconsciously with correct fighting principles.

As well as being an effective fighting and self-defence system, kenpo taiji teaches students to develop and intensify the flow of their own internal energy (chi) by training in chi kung and traditional t'ai chi ch'uan, enabling them to achieve perfect health.
42 _____________ And in addition to that, during the classes some of the greatest martial arts secrets are revealed by Tony.

A If that were the case, the stronger, bigger person would always win.

B As a result of such experiences, more and more people are taking it up.

C This is one of the most formidable street survival, fighting and self-defence systems ever invented.

D Students attending these are taught several training methods.

E If you take it up, you will learn how to get into this condition and you will be able to defend yourself whatever your size, age or gender.

F Many others have now followed his lead.

G Most martial arts are not street effective.

<u>PART 7</u>

You are going to read a magazine article about the best way to see certain artistic masterpieces in various buildings. For questions 43–52, choose from the buildings (A–D). The buildings may be chosen more than once.

Mark your answers on the separate answer sheet.

Of which building are the following stated?

Different categories of visitor are anxious to view the masterpiece. **43**

Some people have the wrong idea about when the building is open. **44**

You may have some difficulty making your arrangements for your visit. **45**

On your return journey through the building, you can look at works of art you missed earlier. **46**

You will be able to get to the masterpiece before other visitors, because they will stop to view other works of art. **47**

Holidaymakers do not normally visit the building but it is an excellent place. **48**

A rule prevents people from viewing the masterpiece for too long. **49**

Make sure you remain in front of the crowds of people as you go through the building. **50**

There is a period when most visitors have left the building. **51**

One suggestion for visiting the building is not as unrealistic as it may appear. **52**

Smart Art

The queue-buster's guide to the world's greatest masterpieces

Early openings, private viewings – here's everything you need for a magic moment with the world's most famous masterpieces

A The Birth of Venus

Uffizi, Florence, Italy

The Florentine master Sandro Botticelli created one of the most graceful and joyful images of the modern age, and the single most popular painting in the Uffizi. To see it at its best, you need to pre-book a ticket for timed entry at 8.15 a.m., courtesy of the Firenze Musei booking service; don't be put off if you can't get through on the phone first time. Once inside, head straight for the suite of rooms 10–14, where the Botticellis are displayed. Then take in the other highlights of the collection – the Da Vincis in room 15, the Raphaels in room 26, and the Caravaggios in room 43 – staying ahead of the hordes as you go. If there are any gaps you want to fill in, work backwards towards the entrance: by now, the crowds will be unavoidable, but you'll have already had the masters to yourself.

B The Death Mask of Tutankhamun

Egyptian Museum, Cairo, Egypt

It is, of course, impossible for one object to embody the vigour and sophistication of ancient Egypt's culture. But the funerary mask of the boy-king Tutankhamun comes close. Eleven kilos of solid gold, inlaid with lapis lazuli, glass paste and semi-precious stones, it's the undisputed star of the Egyptian Museum – which, given the array of mummies, colossi, thrones and jewellery on show here, gives you an idea of its charisma. Whatever the season, there are people clamouring to see it: hefty groups from the cruise liners and Red Sea resorts in the summer and a steady stream of culture-vultures on Nile tours in the cooler months. At least the museum's policy of not allowing guides to stop and talk in front of its display case, in room 3 up on the first floor, means that the flow of visitors doesn't get too congested. But if you want some proper quiet, you need to come at lunchtime. There are fewer independent travellers about, and it's changeover time for the tour parties too. The quietest time is between 11.30 a.m. and 2 p.m. on midweek days in July and August, when the bus tours take all the tourists away for their lunches.

C The Sistine Ceiling

Vatican Museums, Rome, Italy

The really smart way to see Michelangelo's masterwork is on a private tour. At first sight, this looks prohibitively expensive. But form a group of like-minded friends, and suddenly you have the experience of an art-loving lifetime for the price of dinner for two in a posh restaurant. If that's not an option, then you've got to be first in, which means arriving at the vast Vatican Museums complex at least an hour before the doors open, armed with a good map (most Rome guidebooks have them) and a pair of binoculars. Once you're inside, hurry to the chapel – it's at the far end of the complex, and most people will be distracted by some of the other world-class exhibits. The binoculars, by the way, are essential. Michelangelo's forms hover some 20m overhead.

D Girl With A Pearl Earring

Mauritshuis, The Hague, The Netherlands

Vermeer's delicate, deeply ambiguous portrait is one of the most finely observed in all western art. Its home, the Mauristshuis, is some way off the tourist map – even though it's one of the best small museums in Europe – but Dutch school kids make the pilgrimage in droves. A Monday in summer is your best bet for a private view – it's closed that day in winter, and locals assume it's a year-round day off.

Writing (1 hour 20 minutes)

PART 1

*You **must** answer this question. Write your answer in **140–190** words in an appropriate style.*

1   In your English class you have been talking about the importance of sport in people's lives.
Now, your English teacher has asked you to write an essay.
Write an essay using **all** the notes and give reasons for your point of view.

Why is sport important to so many people?

Notes

Write about:

1.   taking part in sport(s)
2.   watch sport(s)
3.   _______________________ (your own idea)

*Write an answer to one of the questions **2–4** in this part. Write your answer in **140–190** words in an appropriate style.*

2   Your college recently staged its annual show, in which students at the college perform. You have been asked to write a review of the show for the college website.

   Write your **review**.

3   You have seen this announcement in an international magazine.

MY FAVOURITE HOBBY

What's your passion when you're not working or studying? Tell us all about it and why you like it. What does it involve? What made you take it up and how much of your time do you spend on it?

We'll publish the best articles in a special section next month.

   Write your **article**.

4   You recently saw this notice in an international magazine.

WHAT ARE THE LATEST FASHIONS WHERE YOU ARE?

We're looking for people to send us reports on the latest fashions among young people in the places where they live. You can tell us about fashions in music, in clothes, in what people buy, in behaviour or anything else you want to describe. And give your opinions on these fashions too. We'll publish some of the reports so that our readers can compare fashions in different places.

   Write your **report**.

Listening (40 minutes)

<u>PART 1</u>

You will hear people talking in eight different situations. For questions 1–8, choose the best answer, (A, B or C).

1   You hear part of an interview with a pop singer.
    How does she feel about what happened?

    A embarrassed by her mistake

    B angry with her tour manager   **1**

    C confused about what happened

2   You hear part of a radio programme for young people.
    What advice does the speaker give?

    A Try to discuss the matter with your friends.

    B Pay no attention to the people who laugh at you.   **2**

    C Encourage other people to be like you.

3   You hear a radio presenter talking about a book.
    What does the presenter say about the book?

    A Some of the writers have already had their work published.

    B It contains work that was entered for a competition.   **3**

    C It is very well organized.

4   You hear someone talking on the phone.
    What is the speaker's purpose?

    A to resolve a disagreement

    B to make a threat   **4**

    C to apologize for previous behaviour

5   You hear someone talking to an assistant at a box office.
    What is the situation?

    A   The man has lost his tickets.

    B   The man was sent the wrong tickets.

    C   The man wants to return the tickets.

5

6   You hear someone talking about her personality.
    What is the speaker doing?

    A   admitting something

    B   explaining something

    C   promising something

6

7   You hear two people talking.
    What is the relationship between them?

    A   They are members of the same club.

    B   They live in the same building.

    C   They are studying on the same course.

7

8   You hear a local radio presenter talking about a competition.
    Which of the following is true of the competition?

    A   The first part does not involve any cooking.

    B   The second part involves ten people cooking on their own.

    C   The final part takes place at a different restaurant.

8

TEST 3

You will hear someone introducing a conference for the organizers of music festivals. For questions 9–18, complete the sentences with a word or short phrase.

CONFERENCE FOR MUSIC FESTIVAL ORGANIZERS

First session

The session will cover disagreements that can happen between festival organizers and

9 _________________________________ .

An expert will give advice on what a 10 _________________________________ should contain.

The session will deal with the issue of 11 _________________________________ at festivals, which affect people's opinions of them.

The session will also focus on how 12 _________________________________ can affect the planning of a festival.

Second session

The session will consider what 13 _________________________________ do in connection with the entertainment provided.

Participants will discuss whether it is a good idea to have competitions that involve a system of

14 _________________________________ .

Third session

The session will focus on how to attract 15 _________________________________ for a festival.

A professional in the area of 16 _________________________________ will address the conference.

Last session

The main topic of the session is ways of 17 _________________________________ festivals.

The practice of having special offers on 18 _________________________________ will also be discussed.

*You will hear five different people talking about what they discovered when they read autobiographies by famous people. For questions **19–23**, choose from the list (**A–H**) what each person says that they discovered. Use the letters only once. There are three extra letters which you do not need to use.*

A He had a terrible life before becoming famous.

Speaker 1   **19**

B He is a nicer person than he appears to be.

Speaker 2   **20**

C He is exactly the same in private as he is in public.

Speaker 3   **21**

D He never intended to become so famous.

Speaker 4   **22**

E He would have preferred a different career.

Speaker 5   **23**

F He was very unkind to other people after he became famous.

G He gets very upset by criticism.

H He feels that he is a very important person.

You will hear an interview with someone whose daughters are appearing in a show in London. For questions 24–30, choose the best answer (A, B or C).

24 What does Jackie say about Olivia's role in *Annie*?

    A Olivia had difficulty learning such a big role.
    B Olivia had always wanted to have such a big role.
    C Olivia hadn't expected to get such a big role.

25 Jackie says that Olivia's performance in *Annie*

    A did not surprise other members of her family.
    B was helped by advice from an agent.
    C contrasted with her normal personality.

26 When Olivia tried to get a part in *Mary Poppins*, she

    A did not really expect to get the part.
    B was extremely upset not to get the part.
    C was immediately rejected for the part.

27 What happened at the first auditions for *The Sound of Music*?

    A Jackie's children were told they would have to come back the next day.
    B The family arrived later than they had been told to arrive.
    C There were so many people that the family considered leaving.

28 For the second audition, both girls

    A decided to wear similar clothes.
    B were required to sing two songs.
    C felt they had to improve.

29 At the final audition,

    A neither of the girls appeared to be nervous.
    B Jackie told them they looked right for the parts.
    C both girls made jokes about the event.

30 How have the girls reacted to getting the parts?

    A They are a bit concerned that their lives will change.
    B The achievement has made them more self-confident.
    C Their behaviour has remained the same as it was before.

Speaking (14 minutes)

PART 1 (2 minutes)

Sport

- What's your favourite sport? ..... (Why?)
- Which sport(s) do you dislike? ..... (Why?)
- Which sports are popular in your country?
- What is your experience of taking part in sports?

The news

- Do you take an interest in what's happening in the news? ..... (Why? / Why not?)
- What newspaper(s) do you read? Describe it / them.
- Apart from newspapers and TV, what other sources of news can you use?
- What's your opinion of the way the media present the news?

Free time

- How much free time do you have?
- What do you like doing during your free time?
- What hobby / hobbies do you have?
- What hobby / hobbies did you have when you were younger?

PART 2 (4 minutes)

1 **Taking photographs**
2 **At the airport**

Candidate A	Look at the two photographs 1A and 1B on page 64. They show people taking photographs. Compare the photographs and say why the person is taking the photograph. *Candidate A talks on his / her own for about 1 minute.*
Candidate B	Which of the photographs being taken do you prefer, and why? *Candidate B talks on his / her own for about 30 seconds.*
Candidate B	Look at the two photographs 2A and 2B on page 64. They show people at airports. Compare the photographs and say what the situation is in each one. *Candidate B talks on his / her own for about 1 minute.*
Candidate A	Which of the people would you prefer to be, and why? *Candidate A talks on his / her own for about 30 seconds.*

PART 2

- Why do you think the person is taking the photograph?

1A

1B

- What is the situation in each photograph?

2A

2B

Planning a local event

PART 3 (4 minutes)

Imagine that a committee is going to organize a one-day event to be enjoyed by people of all ages in the place where you live. Look at the ideas for possible events.

First, talk to each other about why each of these events might be popular.
Then decide which event would be the best one to have.

Candidates A and B discuss this together for about 3 minutes.

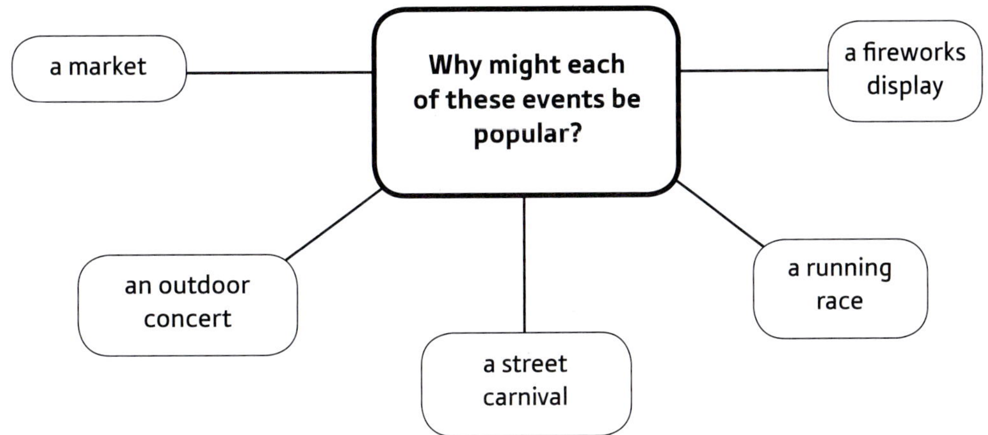

PART 4 (4 minutes)

- What kind of local events take place where you come from? Do young people take part in or attend them?
- Would you like to organize an event like this? ..... (Why? / Why not?)
- What's the best event you've ever attended? Why was it so good?
- What's the worst event you've ever attended? Why was it so bad?
- Do you think that local life is changing where you come from? ..... (Why / Why not?)
- Some people think that in the modern world, local communities are not as important as they used to be. Do you agree?

Reading and Use of English (1 hour 15 minutes)

PART 1

For questions 1–8, read the text below and decide which answer (A, B, C or D) best fits each gap. There is an example at the beginning (0).

Mark your answers on the separate answer sheet.

Example:

0 A notice   **B** attention   **C** regard   **D** interest

0	A	B	C	D

She studies while he plays: true of children and chimps

Little girls watch and learn; little boys don't pay **0**___________ and play around. At least, this seems to be the **1**___________ with chimpanzees, according to new research.

Chimpanzees in the wild **2**___________ to snack on termites, and youngsters learn to fish for them by poking long sticks and other **3**___________ tools into the mounds that large groups of termites build. Researchers found that **4**___________ average female chimps in the Gombe National Park in Tanzania learnt how to do termite fishing at the age of 31 months, more than two years earlier than the males.

The females seem to learn by watching their mothers. Researcher Dr. Elisabeth V. Lonsdorf said that it is **5**___________ to find that, when a young male and female are near a mound, 'she's really focusing on termite fishing and he's spinning himself round **6**___________ circles.' The behaviour of both sexes may seem **7**___________ to many parents, Dr. Lonsdorf said, adding, 'The sex differences we found in the chimps are **8**___________ to some of the findings from human child development research.'

1	**A** case	**B** matter	**C** fact	**D** event
2	**A** delight	**B** enjoy	**C** like	**D** fancy
3	**A** relative	**B** connected	**C** close	**D** similar
4	**A** on	**B** by	**C** at	**D** for
5	**A** ordinary	**B** regular	**C** typical	**D** frequent
6	**A** with	**B** in	**C** to	**D** through
7	**A** acquainted	**B** familiar	**C** recognized	**D** known
8	**A** corresponding	**B** alike	**C** identical	**D** matching

PART 2

*For questions **9–16**, read the text below and think of the word which best fits each gap. Use only* **one** *word in each gap. There is an example at the beginning (**0**).*

Write your answers **IN CAPITAL LETTERS on the separate answer sheet.**

Example:

0	A	T											

NATIONAL VEGETARIAN WEEK

Around 5% of British households now have **0**__________ least one family member who is vegetarian, **9**__________ means that in the region of 3 million British people are vegetarians. Vegetarians do not eat meat, fish or poultry. Among the many reasons **10**__________ being a vegetarian are health, compassion for animals, and religious beliefs.

Statistically, if you choose **11**__________ vegetarian diet, you are choosing an option which should boost your chances of living a long and healthy life. But why? The reason **12**__________ that a good vegetarian diet contains more carbohydrate, more vitamin C and more fibre **13**__________ one where a high proportion of the calories come from meat.

There is documentary evidence of a Vegetarian Day **14**__________ held in Britain as early as 1936, but National Vegetarian Week **15**__________ we know it today has its roots in the National Vegetarian Day held by the Vegetarian Society in October 1991. It proved **16**__________ successful that they extended it to a whole week.

For questions 17–24, read the text below. Use the word given in capitals at the end of some of the lines to form a word that fits in the gap in the same line. There is an example at the beginning (0).

Write your answers IN CAPITAL LETTERS on the separate answer sheet.

Example:

| 0 | L | E | A | D | I | N | G | | | | | | |

WHEN BOSSES MAKE SPEECHES

For business managers, public speaking is part of the job. A survey of

100 **0** _____________ companies found that chief executives received on   **LEAD**

average 175 **17** _____________ a year to speak at conferences. Some   **INVITE**

executives love public speaking but some have an enormous

18 _____________ for it.   **LIKE**

There are plenty of experts giving **19** _____________ to them on how to   **ADVISE**

interest **20** _____________ . According to Carmine Gallo, author of a book   **LISTEN**

on public speaking, it is essential to avoid giving too much information

and to keep the audience's **21** _____________ . He points to the example of   **ATTEND**

one executive whose **22** _____________ involves walking off the stage   **TECHNICAL**

and into the audience, where he asks a question or rests a hand

on a person's shoulder in the style of a television talk-show host.

Speaking without notes, he **23** _____________ that he maintains   **SURE**

constant eye contact with his audience.

And then there was a **24** _____________ public speaker who would   **LEGEND**

gather his ideas before a speech, jotting notes on a pad. People would

ask for a copy of the speech after he had spoken but no such thing existed.

For questions 25–30, complete the second sentence so that it has a similar meaning to the first sentence, using the word given. **Do not change the word given.** *You must use between* **two** *and* **five** *words, including the word given. Here is an example (0).*

Example:

0 Making new friends was easy for her.

   DIFFICULT

   She didn't _________________ new friends.

The gap can be filled with the words 'find it difficult to make', so you write:

<table><tr><td>0</td><td>F I N D I T D I F F I C U L T T O M A K E</td></tr></table>

Write **only** *the missing words* **IN CAPITAL LETTERS on the separate answer sheet.**

---

25 It says here that we should we reply to this invitation.

    SUPPOSED

    It says here that _________________ to this invitation.

26 I haven't got my wallet – it must be at home.

    LEFT

    I haven't got my wallet – I _________________ at home.

27 Is it likely that this invention will become popular with the public?

    CATCH

    Is this invention likely _________________ with the public?

28 There are a minimum of seven classes a week during the course.

    LEAST

    The course consists _________________ seven classes a week.

29 My sister can't drive so she hasn't got her own car.

    KNOW

    My sister _________________ drive so she hasn't got her own car.

30 I wrote down his email address on a piece of paper.

    NOTE

    I _________________ his email address on a piece of paper.

Why I've taken a break from holidays

It is now close to four years since I last took a holiday. This is because I have come to the conclusion, over the course of my adult life, that I am not very good at it. You might think this sounds like saying you're not very good at drinking tea or listening to music. What could possibly be difficult about the natural act of putting your working life on hold for a couple of weeks and going somewhere warm to do nothing?

To be honest, I'm a little baffled myself. I was a model holidaymaker as a kid: every July, I would arrive at an Italian campsite with my parents and, within a couple of days, my skin would have turned an olive colour and I would blend into my surroundings so totally that I would often find myself being mistakenly told to join a party of local schoolchildren. The problems started during my early twenties: a stolen tent and wallet at the Glastonbury Festival in 1995; a lightning strike and sudden drop in altitude on a flight over the Channel in 1997; an ill-fated experiment in 'luxury inter-railing' in 1998 that lasted just four days and ended with the French police mistaking me for a drug smuggler.

But even if I manage to go away without being mugged or getting food poisoning, I now find that I can't really commit to the experience. A fancy-free trip to the South of France five years ago to 'just kind of hang out on the coast' was ended after just two days, mainly because I had an urge to check my e-mails. Similarly, my honeymoon, a year or so later, was cut short by 48 hours – not because my wife and I weren't enjoying ourselves, but because we were missing our cats.

So what is my problem? On the surface, I'm probably a bit of a homebody. And I just find the pressure of being on holiday too severe: it always feels like having a gun held to my head and being forced to have fun. Somehow, packing a carefully itemised list of possessions and meeting a scheduled flight has none of the excitement of suddenly deciding to take a day off and driving somewhere for the fun of it.

Thankfully, I'm not alone. This summer, most of my friends have decided not to have a break. And a recent survey highlighted the downside of holidays, with the results showing that nearly two thirds of people found that the calming effects of a holiday wore off within 24 hours, as stress levels returned to normal. And this year *The Idler* magazine published its *Book of Awful Holidays*. Here you will find a list of the five most ecologically-damaging vacations it's possible to take, along with 50 horrific holiday experiences voted for on *The Idler* website. Over the last decade, *The Idler* has become well known for promoting the idea of an easy, lazy life. The leisure industry might seem an unlikely target of its criticism, but Dan Kiernan, the book's editor, says that he was flooded with entries from readers for his list of Awful Holidays.

'What interests me is what the concept of a "holiday" says about the rest of our lives,' he explains. For me, the point of living is to have a life you enjoy for 52 weeks a year.' **He has a point.** The more I like my life and the better I structure it, the less I want to go away. Maybe I'm weird for not liking holidays, but I just feel my leisure time is too valuable to waste on them.

31 **What does the writer suggest about the fact that he has not taken a holiday for four years?**

    A Some people may find the reason surprising.

    B He often has to explain the reason to other people.

    C There have been times when he has regretted it.

    D It is not something he has thought about before.

32 **What is the writer describing in the second paragraph?**

    A events that explain why he has never really liked holidays

    B events that he regards as not typical of most people's experiences

    C events that illustrate his contrasting experiences of holidays

    D events that he did not consider particularly serious when they happened

33 **The events the writer describes in the third paragraph illustrate**

    A how hard he has tried to enjoy holidays.

    B how badly he behaves when he is on holiday.

    C his fear that something bad will happen when he is on holiday.

    D his lack of enthusiasm for being on holiday.

34 **The writer says in the fourth paragraph that the main thing he dislikes about holidays is that**

    A they are often organized in order to please other people.

    B they are far less enjoyable than breaks that have not been planned in advance.

    C he tends to be made responsible for too much of the organization of them.

    D he feels embarrassed when other people are having fun but he isn't.

35 **The writer says that a recent survey shows that a lot of people**

    A pretend to enjoy their holidays.

    B fail to relax while they are on holiday.

    C feel that the benefits of going on holiday are limited.

    D have made the same decision as the writer and most of his friends.

36 **The writer says that the book published by *The Idler* magazine**

    A illustrates a point that the magazine has often made.

    B proved more popular than he would have expected.

    C focuses entirely on bad personal experiences of holidays.

    D indicates that his dislike of holidays is widely shared.

You are going to read an article about maps showing the homes of film stars. Six sentences have been removed from the article. Choose from the sentences A–G the one which fits each gap (37–42). There is one extra sentence which you do not need to use.

Mark your answers **on the separate answer sheet.**

Maps of the stars

Ever since the 1910s, when film-makers like Cecil B. DeMille first set up shop in Hollywood, mapmakers, the explorers of the city's social terrain, have been compiling that only-in-Los Angeles fixture, maps showing the locations of the fabulous homes of the stars. Collectively, they form an unofficial version of the Oscars, reflecting who's in and who's out in the film world. 'Each one looks different,' says Linda Welton, whose grandfather and mother pioneered these maps. **37** _____________ Former icons vanish from them, new ones appear on them, and some of the truly greats are permanent fixtures on them.

In 1933, noticing the steady stream of tourists drifting westward to follow the stars from Hollywood to Beverly Hills, the nearby district where most of the stars went to live, Ms Welton's grandfather, Wesley G Lake, obtained a copyright for his *Guide to Starland Estates and Mansions*. **38** _____________ For 40 years Ms Welton's mother, Vivienne E Welton, sold maps just down the road from Gary Cooper's place at 200 Baroda*. The asterisk indicates that it was the actor's final home, as opposed to a plus sign (denoting a former home) or a zero (for no view from the street).

'My grandfather asked Mom to talk to the gardeners to find out where the stars lived,' Ms Welton recalls. 'She'd say: "Oh, this is a beautiful garden. Who lives here?" Who would suspect a little girl?' Ms Welton and her crew now sell about 10,000 maps a year from a folding chair parked curbside six days a week. **39** _____________

The evolution of the maps mirrors both the Hollywood publicity machine and real estate and tourism development. **40** _____________ The first celebrity home, according to Marc Wanamaker, a historian and a founder of the Westwood and Beverly Hills Historical Societies, belonged to the artist Paul de Longpre. He had a luxuriously-landscaped house at Cahuenga Avenue and Hollywood and real estate

agents would take prospective clients past it on tours.

Although it is not known for certain who published the first map, by the mid-1920s all sorts of people were producing them. **41** _____________

One of the most famous of the early maps was produced to show the location of Pickfair, the sprawling home of the newly married stars Mary Pickford and Douglas Fairbanks Sr, and the homes of some of their star friends. During World War I, they opened their home to serve refreshments to soldiers. As Vivienne Welton once explained in an interview with *Mercator's World*, a map and cartography magazine, 'She urged a few friends to do the same. **42** _____________'

For over 40 years, people have marched toward the corner of Sunset and Baroda with hand-painted yellow signs saying: 'Star Maps, 2 blocks', 'Star Maps, 1 block', 'Star Maps here'. The maps reflect the shifting geography of stardom as celebrities, seeking escape from over-enthusiastic fans, some with ill intentions, have moved out to other locations.

A   As they do so, they give advice to the tourists on star safaris through the lime green landscape of Beverly Hills.

B   Studios like Paramount published the names and addresses of its stars on theirs, and businesses distributed them as a promotional gimmick.

C   Others, however, say that the star maps are still an essential part of Hollywood and the film world.

D   Early film stars like Lillian Gish lived in modest, somewhat grubby rooming houses, taking street cars to and from the studio.

E   Updated regularly, they are still for sale at the corner of Sunset Boulevard and Baroda Drive.

F   And so a map was needed.

G   It is the oldest continuously published star map and one of a half-dozen or so maps of varying degrees of accuracy and spelling correctness sold today.

PART 7

*You are going to read a magazine article about baseball. For questions **43–52**, choose from the sections of the article (**A–F**). The sections may be chosen more than once. When more than one answer is required, these may be given in any order.*

Mark your answers **on the separate answer sheet.**

In which section of the article are the following mentioned?

the reason why a false story about the history of baseball was made public	**43**
a past belief that it was not worth keeping records on matters such as baseball	**44**
the importance of baseball in people's lives	**45**
the discovery of a document indicating that baseball existed even earlier than had previously been thought	**46**
uncertainty as to what future investigations of the origins of baseball will focus on	**47**
a belief that the true origin of baseball might never be firmly established	**48**
a belief that baseball developed gradually rather than having a single starting point	**49**
a contrast between what is known about baseball and what is known about well-known people in US history	**50**
the enormous importance of facts and records in baseball	**51**
the identification of an individual who was claimed to be the inventor of baseball	**52**

The origins of baseball

A Textbooks once stated with complete certainty that baseball was invented in Cooperstown, New York, in 1839, and provided as proof the picture of a dusty, ripped ball pulled from an attic trunk. It turned out to be a hoax. The next official version put the origin in Hoboken, New Jersey, in 1846. That story stood until 2001, when a librarian found two 1823 newspaper references to baseball games in Lower Manhattan. Then, in May 2004, a clerk walked out of a library vault in Pittsfield, Massachusetts, waving a faded ordinance from 1791 that banned the playing of baseball within 72 meters of the big church in the town square.

B For baseball, there is no agreement on which century the first game was played. It could have been the 18th century; it could have been the 13th century. There is some record of each. There is no agreement on which continent baseball was invented in. Was it North America, Europe or Africa? There is evidence for all three. 'With a sport like baseball, which so cares about statistics and its past,' the historian Doris Kearnes Goodwin said, 'you would think that this major detail of the past would be the crown jewel to find. Baseball, after all, is the ultimate sport of figures and dates. The origin of the game is the fabulous treasure.'

C 'People ask: when was the first baseball game?' said John Thorn, the baseball historian who uncovered the existence of the Pittsfield ordinance during a middle-of-the-night Internet search. 'It may be an unanswerable question. That's what makes it eternally fascinating.' Ted Spencer, long-time curator at the National Baseball Hall of Fame in Cooperstown, New York, added another perspective. 'Did you know the Pittsfield ordinance also bans another bunch of sports, including football?' Mr. Spencer said. 'Did you know nobody cares? But they care that it mentioned baseball. I got calls from reporters all over the country. That's because baseball has a spiritual hold on the American public.'

D The most commonly accepted theory is that baseball has no specific starting date or place of invention. The game, they say, evolved over time. Still, it does raise some fundamental questions: Why has baseball's earliest history been so undiscovered? Why is it that the small details of the lives of celebrated American pioneers are so public but until recently little was done to trace baseball before 1823? 'Because the daily lives of prominent leaders in the American colonies were considered important and someone wrote the details down,' said Mr Shieber, the Hall of Fame's new media curator. 'But the games were child's play and often regarded as a wasteful use of time. They weren't documented in the same way.'

E Placing the origin of baseball in Cooperstown in 1839 was the work of a turn-of-the-century commission empowered by A.G. Spalding, the sports goods businessman, who influenced the findings to ensure the sport had, in his words at the time, 'an American dad'. That became Doubleday, an officer during the American Civil War, who was supposed to have laid out the first baseball field in Cooperstown. In the latter half of the 20th century, this tale was totally discredited.

F At the Hall of Fame, Mr. Spencer pointed to a reproduction hanging on a wall. It is a drawing from Spain in 1251 of people playing a game. 'There's a bat and there's a ball,' he said, looking at the drawing. 'It looks like two guys playing baseball to me.' Not far away is another reproduction of an Egyptian wall inscription: pharaohs perhaps engaged in another ball game. 'I guess the searching could go in any direction,' Ms. Goodwin said.

Writing (1 hour 20 minutes)

PART 1

*You **must** answer this question. Write your answer in 140–190 words in an appropriate style.*

1   In your English class you have been talking about careers and choosing them. Now, your English teacher has asked you to write an essay. Write an essay using **all** the notes and give reasons for your point of view.

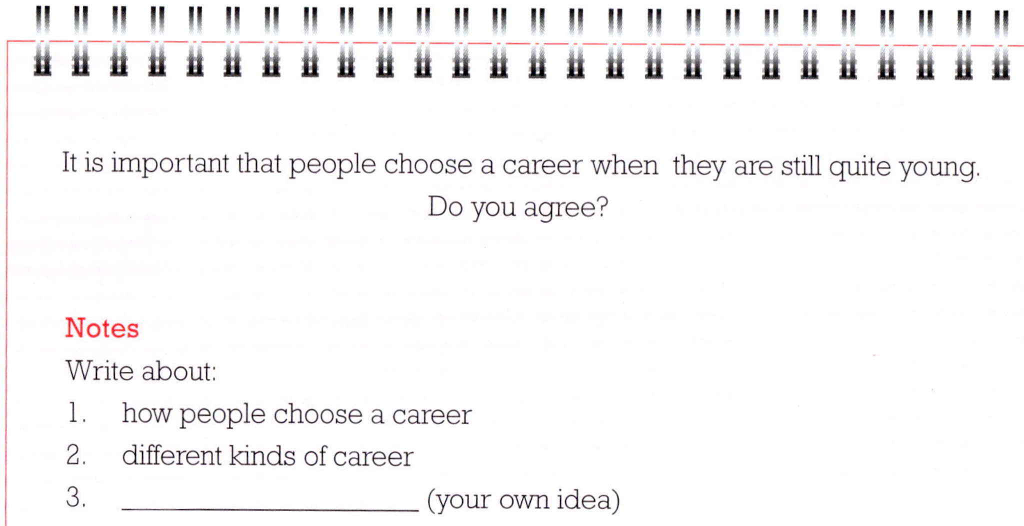

Write an answer to one of the questions 2–4 in this part. Write your answer in 140–190 words in an appropriate style.

---

2   You recently saw this notice in an English-language magazine.

> ### THE GAMES PEOPLE PLAY
>
> Write a review of a game that you played recently. It doesn't have to be a new game. You could review a computer game, or any other indoor game such as a board game. Describe the game and give us your opinions on it. Is it exciting? Is it hard to be good at it? If it's a popular game, why is it popular, in your opinion? We'll publish some of the reviews in a special section about games around the world.

Write your **review**.

3   You have seen this announcement in an English-language magazine.

> ### ARE YOU A WINNER?
>
> Have you ever entered a competition or a sports tournament? Write and tell us about your experiences. Tell us about the competition or tournament. Did you enjoy it? Did you expect to win? Did you win? If so, what was the prize? If not, how did you feel? We'll publish the best letters in a special Letters Page.

Write your **letter**.

4   Your English teacher has asked you to write a report on tourism in your city / region. You should include information on what tourists can do when they visit.

Write your **report**.

Listening (40 minutes)

PART 1

You will hear people talking in eight different situations. For questions 1–8, choose the best answer, (A, B or C).

1 You hear someone talking on a radio programme.
  What is the speaker doing?

  A recommending that listeners make a certain drink

  B explaining why a drink is becoming more popular

  C telling listeners about a drink they may not know about

2 You hear someone talking about people who travel a lot when they're young.
  What is his attitude towards these people?

  A He is envious of them for having the opportunity.

  B He feels that they are simply wasting their time.

  C He can't understand why they do it.

3 You hear an advertisement for a course.
  What does the speaker say about the course?

  A You need to take a test before being accepted for it.

  B It starts with theory and moves on to practical work.

  C It focuses on your effect on the people you will instruct.

4 You hear part of a radio interview.
  Who is being interviewed?

  A a film director

  B an actor

  C a screenwriter

5   You hear part of a radio report about car drivers.
    What did the survey discover about a lot of drivers?

    A   They pay no attention to warning lights.

    B   They don't know what various symbols in a car relate to.   **5**

    C   They think there are too many warning lights and symbols in cars.

6   You turn on the radio and hear part of a programme.
    What type of programme is it?

    A   a review programme

    B   a chat show   **6**

    C   a phone-in

7   You hear part of a radio play.
    Where is the scene taking place?

    A   in a restaurant

    B   in a car   **7**

    C   in a house

8   You hear a woman talking about running.
    What aspect of running is she talking about?

    A   her involvement in running over a period of time

    B   why she finds running so enjoyable   **8**

    C   the importance of running and training with others

You will hear an announcement about a competition. For questions 9–18, complete the sentences with a word or short phrase.

THE IDEAS COMPETITION

The money given to the winner is not a **9** _______________________________ .

The winner might be **10** _______________________________ with a plan for improving a water supply.

The winner might have an idea about how to help the **11** _______________________________ in the world.

If you enter the competition by phone you must explain your idea in a maximum of **12** _______________________________ .

One of the categories is for people who want to start a business that provides a **13** _______________ or _______________ that currently doesn't exist.

One of the categories is for people who want to take part in a project that is **14** _______________________________ .

One of the rules is that **15** _______________________________ for the competition are not allowed.

Before you phone, it may be a good idea to prepare a **16** _______________________________ .

To win, you must show that you have a lot of **17** _______________________________ for your idea.

Judges will listen to the ideas presented by **18** _______________________________ people.

You will hear five different people talking about how they felt when they received an award. For questions 19–23, choose from the list (A–H) how each person felt. Use the letters only once. There are three extra letters which you do not need to use.

A relieved

Speaker 1   **19**

B worried

Speaker 2   **20**

C proud

Speaker 3   **21**

D exhausted

Speaker 4   **22**

E embarrassed

Speaker 5   **23**

F grateful

G confused

H amused

PART 4

You will hear an interview with someone who has started a magazine for children. For questions 24–30, choose the best answer (A, B or C).

24 When talking about her job as a primary school teacher, Kate emphasizes
   A how much effort the job required.
   B how good she was as a teacher.
   C how difficult the children could be.

   24

25 Kate decided to start her own magazine for children
   A because both children and parents suggested the idea.
   B when she was working in publishing for children.
   C after considering what was available for children.

   25

26 What does Kate say about enthusiasm?
   A Children respond positively to it.
   B Children cannot maintain it for long.
   C Children experience it more than adults.

   26

27 Kate says that she learnt from her research that children
   A don't want to feel that they are being considered inferior.
   B don't like texts that have too much serious content.
   C don't know some words that she had expected them to know.

   27

28 Kate says that the age range for the magazine
   A may change to some extent in the future.
   B may not be exactly what it is stated to be.
   C has been decided after asking parents.

   28

29 Kate says that the magazine makes use of the Internet because
   A some children prefer using it to learn about subjects.
   B some subjects cannot be covered fully in the magazine.
   C it is used a great deal in connection with some school work.

   29

30 Kate says that one of her aims for the magazine is to
   A include subjects that children don't normally read about.
   B create an interest in subjects some children consider boring.
   C encourage children to choose what they want as a career.

   30

Speaking (14 minutes)

PART 1 (2 minutes)

Music

- What's your favourite kind of music? ..... (Why?)
- What kind(s) of music don't you like? ..... (Why?)
- What kinds of music are popular with young people in your country? ..... (Why?)
- Have you ever tried to play a musical instrument? Did you do well?

Technology / Gadgets

- What pieces of technology or electronic gadgets do you own?
- How did you learn how to use pieces of technology or electronic gadgets?
- What do you think are the advantages and disadvantages of new technology for communicating with other people? ..... (Why?)
- Which pieces of technology or electronic gadgets would you like to own? ..... (Why?)

Books and reading

- Do you spend a lot of time reading? ..... (Why? / Why not?)
- What kind of books do you particularly like reading?
- Describe the last book that you read.
- Apart from books, what kind of things do you read?

PART 2 (4 minutes)

1 Working life
2 Visiting a city

Candidate A	Look at the two photographs 1A and 1B on page 84. They show people working. Compare the photographs and say what the people's working lives are like. *Candidate A talks on his / her own for about 1 minute.*
Candidate B	Which of the situations would you prefer to be in, and why? *Candidate B talks on his / her own for about 30 seconds.*
Candidate B	Look at the two photographs 2A and 2B on page 84. They show visitors to a city. Compare the photographs and say what kind of trips the people are on. *Candidate B talks on his / her own for about 1 minute.*
Candidate A	Which of the trips would you prefer to take? *Candidate A talks on his / her own for about 30 seconds.*

- What are the people's working lives like?

1A

1B

- What kind of trips are the people on?

2A

2B

A day with a visitor

PART 3 (4 minutes)

Imagine that a friend of yours has a friend from another country staying with him / her. Your friend has to go out for a day next week and has asked you to look after the visitor for a day. Look at the ideas for what you could do with the visitor for that day.

First, talk to each other about which of the activities would be good for the visitor and good for you.

Then decide which two activities to do with the visitor and plan the day.

Candidates A and B discuss this together for about 3 minutes.

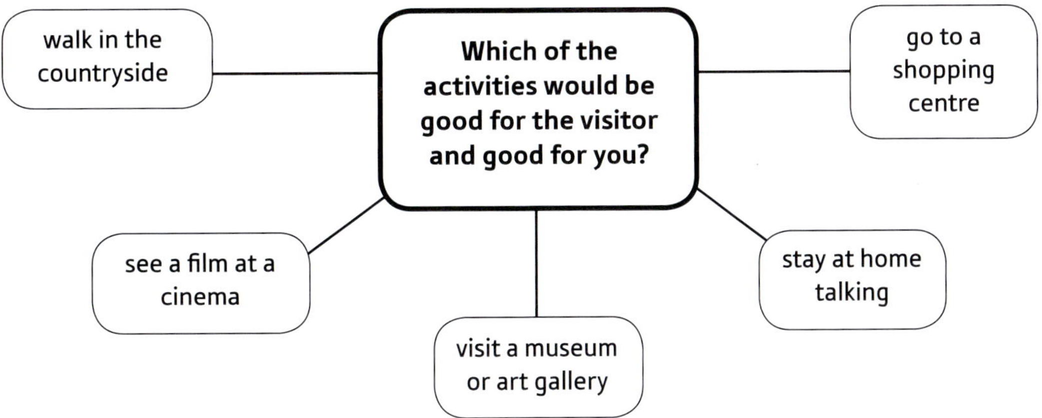

PART 4 (4 minutes)

- If a visitor from another country came to stay with you, what would be the first place you would take that person to? ..... (Why?)
- What place(s) would you certainly not take a visitor to? ..... (Why?)
- Do many overseas visitors come to your country? ..... (Why? / Why not?)
- When you go out with friends, what sort of places do you go to and what do you do there?
- How active are young people in your country? Do they prefer to do things that involve sitting down for long periods?
- What entertainment is available in the place where you live? What other kinds of entertainment do you think should be available?
- Some people say that too much entertainment is available to people and so they are unable to entertain themselves. Do you agree?

Cambridge English: First   Practice Test 1

Name ....

READING AND USE OF ENGLISH

PART 1: Mark ONE letter for each question.

1	A	B	C	D		5	A	B	C	D
2	A	B	C	D		6	A	B	C	D
3	A	B	C	D		7	A	B	C	D
4	A	B	C	D		8	A	B	C	D

PART 2: Write your answers clearly IN CAPITAL LETTERS. Write one letter in each box.

9
10
11
12
13
14
15
16

PART 3: Write your answers clearly IN CAPITAL LETTERS. Write one letter in each box.

17
18
19
20
21
22
23
24

PART 4: Write only the missing words IN CAPITAL LETTERS.

25
26
27
28
29
30

PART 5: Mark ONE letter for each question.

31	A	B	C	D		34	A	B	C	D
32	A	B	C	D		35	A	B	C	D
33	A	B	C	D		36	A	B	C	D

PART 6: Mark ONE letter for each question.

37	A	B	C	D	E	F	G		40	A	B	C	D	E	F	G
38	A	B	C	D	E	F	G		41	A	B	C	D	E	F	G
39	A	B	C	D	E	F	G		42	A	B	C	D	E	F	G

PART 7: Mark ONE letter for each question.

43	A	B	C	D		48	A	B	C	D
44	A	B	C	D		49	A	B	C	D
45	A	B	C	D		50	A	B	C	D
46	A	B	C	D		51	A	B	C	D
47	A	B	C	D		52	A	B	C	D

LISTENING

PART 1: Mark ONE letter for each question.

1	A	B	C		5	A	B	C
2	A	B	C		6	A	B	C
3	A	B	C		7	A	B	C
4	A	B	C		8	A	B	C

PART 2: Write your answers clearly IN CAPITAL LETTERS. Write one letter in each box.

9	
10	
11	
12	
13	
14	
15	
16	
17	
18	

PART 3: Mark ONE letter for each question.

19	A	B	C	D	E	F	G	H
20	A	B	C	D	E	F	G	H
21	A	B	C	D	E	F	G	H
22	A	B	C	D	E	F	G	H
23	A	B	C	D	E	F	G	H

PART 4: Mark ONE letter for each question.

24	A	B	C		28	A	B	C
25	A	B	C		29	A	B	C
26	A	B	C		30	A	B	C
27	A	B	C

Cambridge English: First Practice Test 2

Name ....

READING AND USE OF ENGLISH

PART 1: Mark ONE letter for each question.

1	A	B	C	D		5	A	B	C	D
2	A	B	C	D		6	A	B	C	D
3	A	B	C	D		7	A	B	C	D
4	A	B	C	D		8	A	B	C	D

PART 2: Write your answers clearly IN CAPITAL LETTERS. Write one letter in each box.

9
10
11
12
13
14
15
16

PART 3: Write your answers clearly IN CAPITAL LETTERS. Write one letter in each box.

17
18
19
20
21
22
23
24

PART 4: Write only the missing words IN CAPITAL LETTERS.

25
26
27
28
29
30

PART 5: Mark ONE letter for each question.

31	A	B	C	D		34	A	B	C	D
32	A	B	C	D		35	A	B	C	D
33	A	B	C	D		36	A	B	C	D

PART 6: Mark ONE letter for each question.

37	A	B	C	D	E	F	G
38	A	B	C	D	E	F	G
39	A	B	C	D	E	F	G

40	A	B	C	D	E	F	G
41	A	B	C	D	E	F	G
42	A	B	C	D	E	F	G

PART 7: Mark ONE letter for each question.

43	A	B	C	D
44	A	B	C	D
45	A	B	C	D
46	A	B	C	D
47	A	B	C	D

48	A	B	C	D
49	A	B	C	D
50	A	B	C	D
51	A	B	C	D
52	A	B	C	D

LISTENING

PART 1: Mark ONE letter for each question.

1	A	B	C
2	A	B	C
3	A	B	C
4	A	B	C

5	A	B	C
6	A	B	C
7	A	B	C
8	A	B	C

PART 2: Write your answers clearly IN CAPITAL LETTERS. Write one letter in each box.

9																						
10																						
11																						
12																						
13																						
14																						
15																						
16																						
17																						
18																						

PART 3: Mark ONE letter for each question.

19	A	B	C	D	E	F	G	H
20	A	B	C	D	E	F	G	H
21	A	B	C	D	E	F	G	H
22	A	B	C	D	E	F	G	H
23	A	B	C	D	E	F	G	H

PART 4: Mark ONE letter for each question.

24	A	B	C
25	A	B	C
26	A	B	C
27	A	B	C

28	A	B	C
29	A	B	C
30	A	B	C

Cambridge English: First Practice Test 3

Name ....

READING AND USE OF ENGLISH

PART 1: Mark ONE letter for each question.

1	A	B	C	D
2	A	B	C	D
3	A	B	C	D
4	A	B	C	D

5	A	B	C	D
6	A	B	C	D
7	A	B	C	D
8	A	B	C	D

PART 2: Write your answers clearly IN CAPITAL LETTERS. Write one letter in each box.

9																				
10																				
11																				
12																				
13																				
14																				
15																				
16																				

PART 3: Write your answers clearly IN CAPITAL LETTERS. Write one letter in each box.

17																				
18																				
19																				
20																				
21																				
22																				
23																				
24																				

PART 4: Write only the missing words IN CAPITAL LETTERS.

25	
26	
27	
28	
29	
30	

PART 5: Mark ONE letter for each question.

31	A	B	C	D
32	A	B	C	D
33	A	B	C	D

34	A	B	C	D
35	A	B	C	D
36	A	B	C	D

PHOTOCOPIABLE

PART 6: Mark ONE letter for each question.

37	A	B	C	D	E	F	G
38	A	B	C	D	E	F	G
39	A	B	C	D	E	F	G

40	A	B	C	D	E	F	G
41	A	B	C	D	E	F	G
42	A	B	C	D	E	F	G

PART 7: Mark ONE letter for each question.

43	A	B	C	D
44	A	B	C	D
45	A	B	C	D
46	A	B	C	D
47	A	B	C	D

48	A	B	C	D
49	A	B	C	D
50	A	B	C	D
51	A	B	C	D
52	A	B	C	D

LISTENING

PART 1: Mark ONE letter for each question.

1	A	B	C
2	A	B	C
3	A	B	C
4	A	B	C

5	A	B	C
6	A	B	C
7	A	B	C
8	A	B	C

PART 2: Write your answers clearly IN CAPITAL LETTERS. Write one letter in each box.

9	
10	
11	
12	
13	
14	
15	
16	
17	
18	

PART 3: Mark ONE letter for each question.

19	A	B	C	D	E	F	G	H
20	A	B	C	D	E	F	G	H
21	A	B	C	D	E	F	G	H
22	A	B	C	D	E	F	G	H
23	A	B	C	D	E	F	G	H

PART 4: Mark ONE letter for each question.

24	A	B	C
25	A	B	C
26	A	B	C
27	A	B	C

28	A	B	C
29	A	B	C
30	A	B	C

Cambridge English: First Practice Test 4

Name ....

READING AND USE OF ENGLISH

PART 1: Mark ONE letter for each question.

PART 2: Write your answers clearly IN CAPITAL LETTERS. Write one letter in each box.

9	
10	
11	
12	
13	
14	
15	
16	

PART 3: Write your answers clearly IN CAPITAL LETTERS. Write one letter in each box.

17	
18	
19	
20	
21	
22	
23	
24	

PART 4: Write only the missing words IN CAPITAL LETTERS.

25	
26	
27	
28	
29	
30	

PART 5: Mark ONE letter for each question.

PART 6: Mark ONE letter for each question.

37	A	B	C	D	E	F	G
38	A	B	C	D	E	F	G
39	A	B	C	D	E	F	G

40	A	B	C	D	E	F	G
41	A	B	C	D	E	F	G
42	A	B	C	D	E	F	G

PART 7: Mark ONE letter for each question.

43	A	B	C	D
44	A	B	C	D
45	A	B	C	D
46	A	B	C	D
47	A	B	C	D

48	A	B	C	D
49	A	B	C	D
50	A	B	C	D
51	A	B	C	D
52	A	B	C	D

LISTENING

PART 1: Mark ONE letter for each question.

1	A	B	C
2	A	B	C
3	A	B	C
4	A	B	C

5	A	B	C
6	A	B	C
7	A	B	C
8	A	B	C

PART 2: Write your answers clearly IN CAPITAL LETTERS. Write one letter in each box.

9																								
10																								
11																								
12																								
13																								
14																								
15																								
16																								
17																								
18																								

PART 3: Mark ONE letter for each question.

19	A	B	C	D	E	F	G	H
20	A	B	C	D	E	F	G	H
21	A	B	C	D	E	F	G	H
22	A	B	C	D	E	F	G	H
23	A	B	C	D	E	F	G	H

PART 4: Mark ONE letter for each question.

24	A	B	C
25	A	B	C
26	A	B	C
27	A	B	C

28	A	B	C
29	A	B	C
30	A	B	C

Assessing the Writing paper

Students' answers are assessed using a mark scheme which was developed with close reference to the Common European Framework of Reference for Languages (CEFR). Marks are awarded from 0 to 5 on each of the following four scales:

Content focuses on how well the candidate has fulfilled the task, in other words if they have done what they were asked to do.

Communicative achievement focuses on how appropriate the writing is for the task and whether the candidate has used the appropriate register.

Organization focuses on the way the candidate puts together the piece of writing, in other words if it is logical and ordered.

Language focuses on vocabulary and grammar. This includes the range of language as well as how accurate it is.

Tasks on the *Cambridge English: First* Writing paper are assessed using the following scale, based on B2 of the CEFR:

B2	Content	Communicative Achievement	Organization	Language
5	All content is relevant to the task. Target reader is fully informed.	Uses the conventions of the communicative task effectively to hold the target reader's attention and communicate straightforward and complex ideas, as appropriate.	Text is well-organized and coherent, using a variety of cohesive devices and organizational patterns to generally good effect.	Uses a range of vocabulary, including less common lexis, appropriately. Uses a range of simple and complex grammatical forms with control and flexibility. Occasional errors may be present but do not impede communication.
4	*Performance shares features of Bands 3 and 5.*			
3	Minor irrelevances and/or omissions may be present. Target reader is on the whole informed.	Uses the conventions of the communicative task to hold the target reader's attention and communicate straightforward ideas.	Text is generally well-organized and coherent, using a variety of linking words and cohesive devices.	Uses a range of everyday vocabulary appropriately, with occasional inappropriate use of less common lexis. Uses a range of simple and some complex grammatical forms with a good degree of control. Errors do not impede communication.
2	*Performance shares features of Bands 1 and 3.*			
1	Irrelevances and misinterpretation of task may be present. Target reader is minimally informed.	Uses the conventions of the communicative task in generally appropriate ways to communicate straightforward ideas.	Text is connected and coherent, using basic linking words and a limited number of cohesive devices.	Uses everyday vocabulary generally appropriately, while occasionally overusing certain lexis. Uses simple grammatical forms with a good degree of control. While errors are noticeable, meaning can still be determined.
0	Content is totally irrelevant. Target reader is not informed.	*Performance below Band 1*		